GREAT JAZZ STANDARDS

ISBN 0-7935-3308-2

CORPORATION
7777 W. BLUEMOUND RD. P.O. BOX 13819 MILWAUKEE, WI 53213

Visit Hal Leonard Online at
www.halleonard.com

ALL THE THINGS YOU ARE

from VERY WARM FOR MAY

Lyrics by OSCAR HAMMERSTEIN II
Music by JEROME KERN

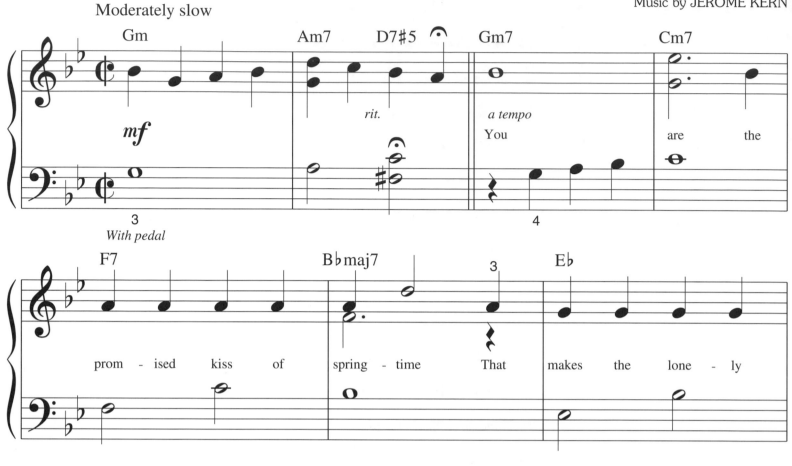

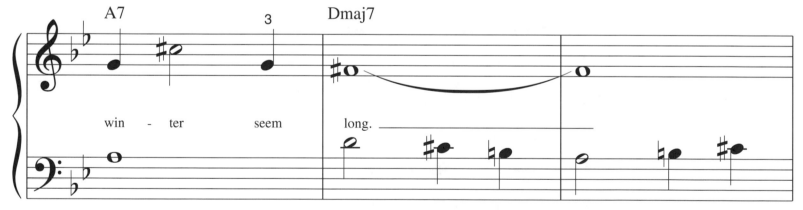

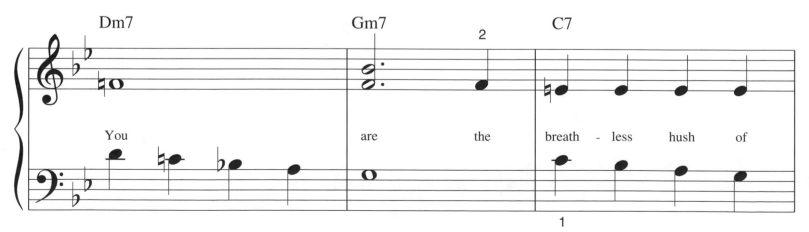

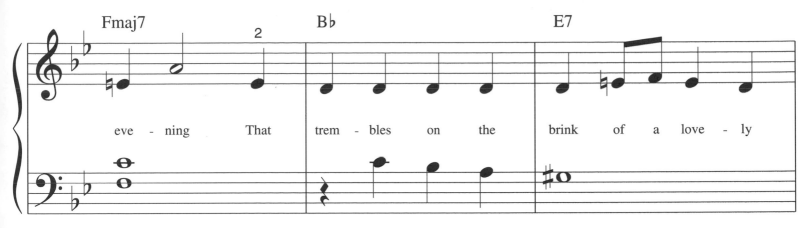

eve - ning That trem - bles on the brink of a love - ly

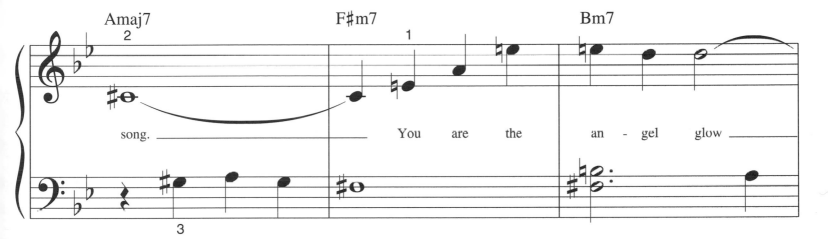

song. _____ You are the an - gel glow _____

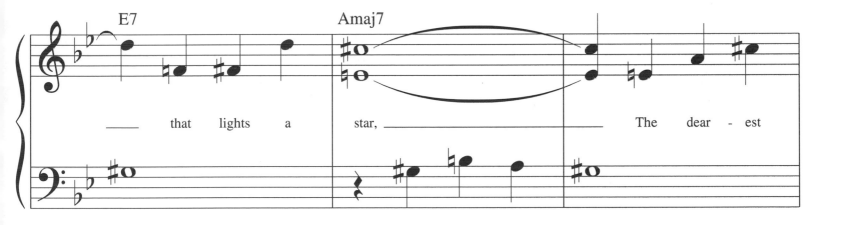

_____ that lights a star, _____ The dear - est

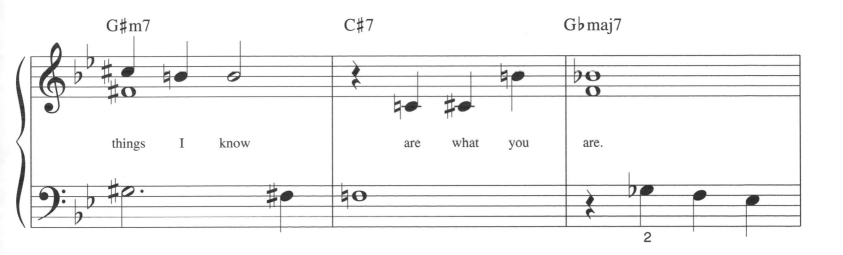

things I know are what you are.

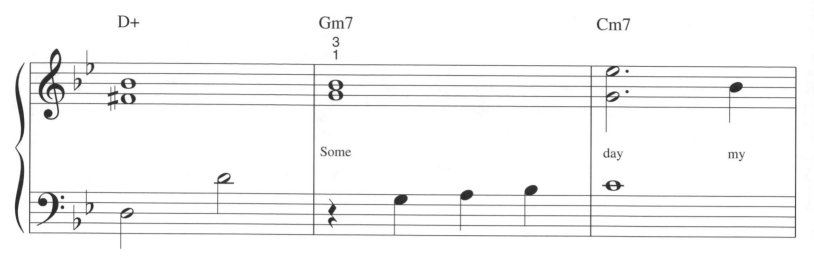

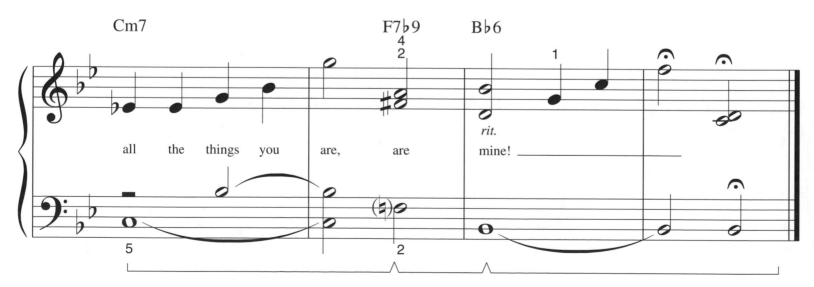

APRIL IN PARIS

Words E.Y. HARBURG
Music by VERNON DUKE

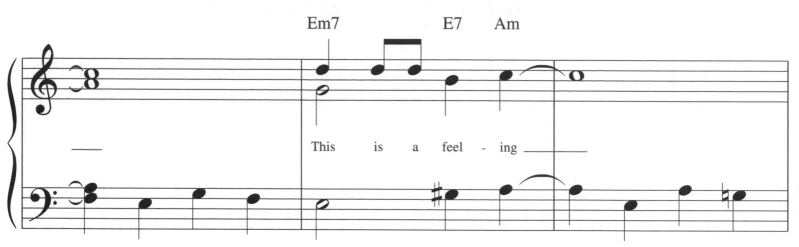

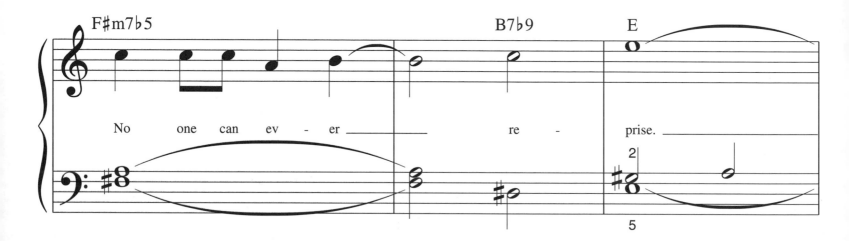

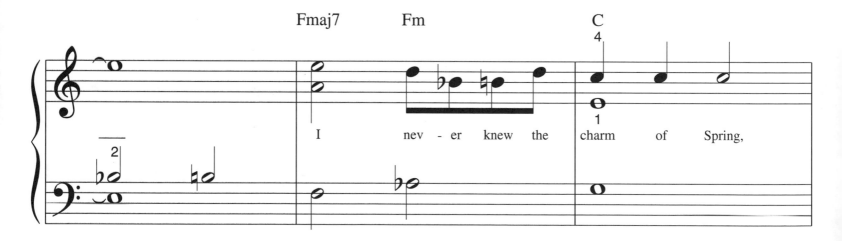

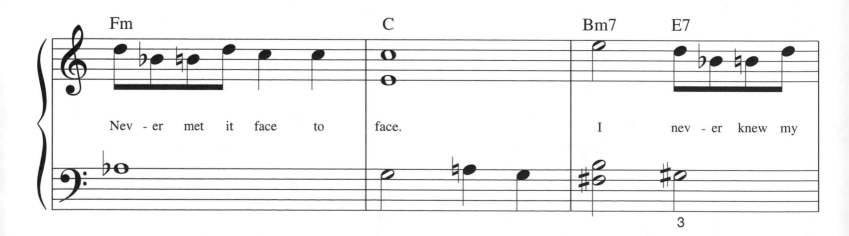

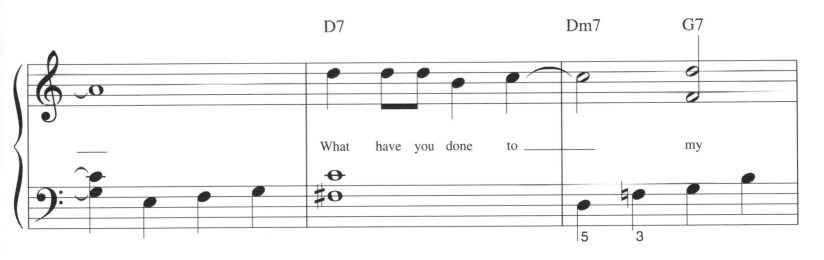

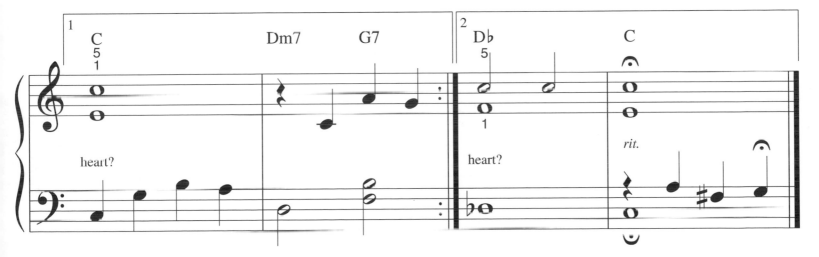

AUTUMN LEAVES

English lyric by JOHNNY MERCER
French lyric by JACQUES PREVERT
Music by JOSEPH KOSMA

Oh! je vou - drais tant que tu te sou - viennes,
Les Feuil - les Mortes se ra - massent à la pelle,

des jours heu - reux où nous é - tions a - mis. En ce temps - là la vie
les sou - ve - nirs et les re - grets aus - si. Mais mon a - mour si - len -

é - tait plus belle et le so - leil plus brû - lant qu'au - jourd - 'hui.
cieux et fi - dèle sou - rit tou - jours et re - mer - cie la vie.

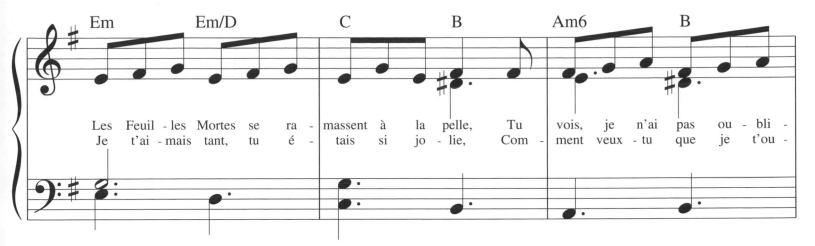

Les Feuil - les Mortes se ra - massent à la pelle, Tu vois, je n'ai pas ou - bli -
Je t'ai - mais tant, tu é - tais si jo - lie, Com - ment veux - tu que je t'ou -

é. Les Feuil - les Mortes se ra - massent à la pelle
blie. En ce temps - là la vie è - tait plus belle

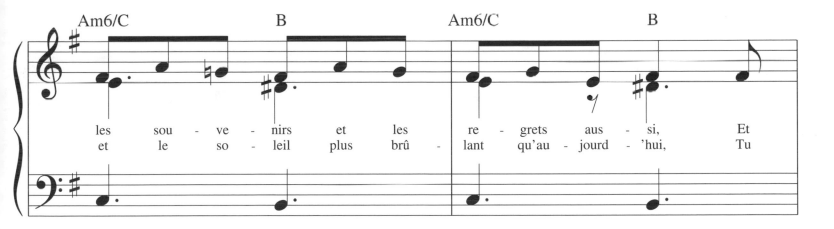

les sou - ve - nirs et les re - grets aus - si, Et
et le so - leil plus brû - lant qu'au - jourd - 'hui, Tu

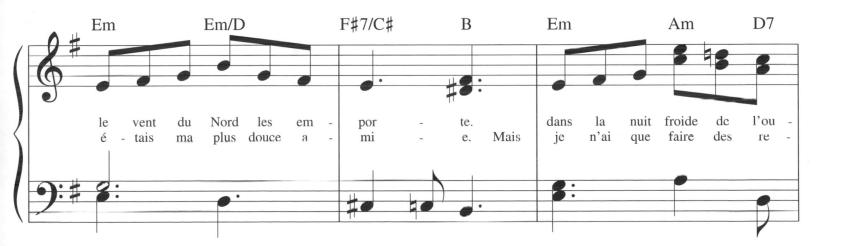

le vent du Nord les em - por - te. dans la nuit froide de l'ou -
é - tais ma plus douce a - mi - e. Mais je n'ai que faire des re -

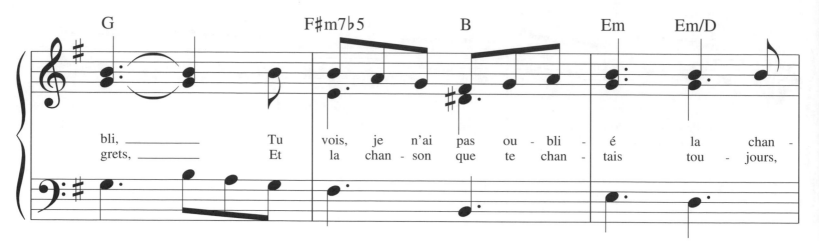

bli, _____ Tu vois, je n'ai pas ou - bli - é la chan -
grets, _____ Et la chan - son que te chan - tais tou - jours,

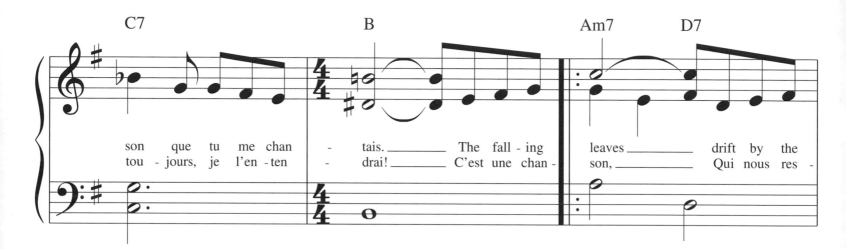

son que tu me chan - tais. _____ The fall - ing leaves _____ drift by the
tou - jours, je l'en -ten - drai! _____ C'est une chan - son, _____ Qui nous res -

win - dow, _____ the au - tumn leaves _____ of red and
sem - ble, _____ Toi tu m'ai - mais _____ Et je t'ai

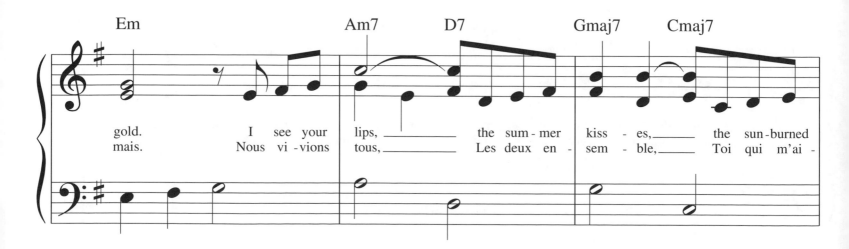

gold. I see your lips, _____ the sum - mer kiss - es, _____ the sun-burned
mais. Nous vi -vions tous, _____ Les deux en - sem - ble, _____ Toi qui m'ai -

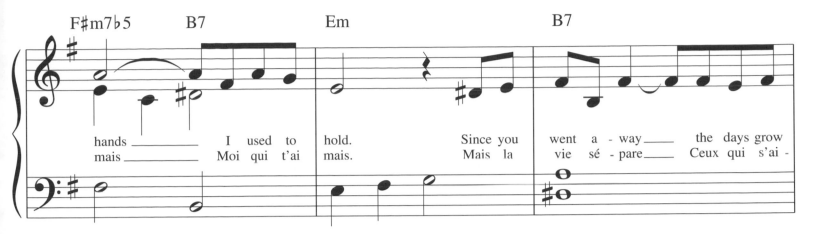

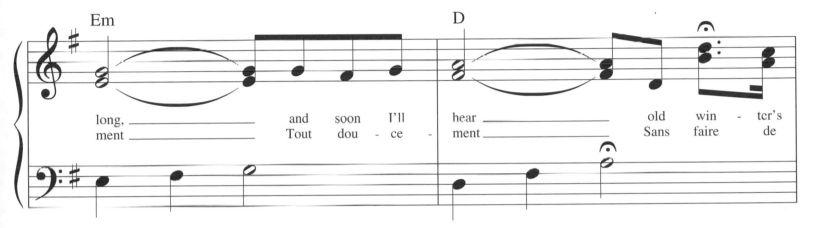

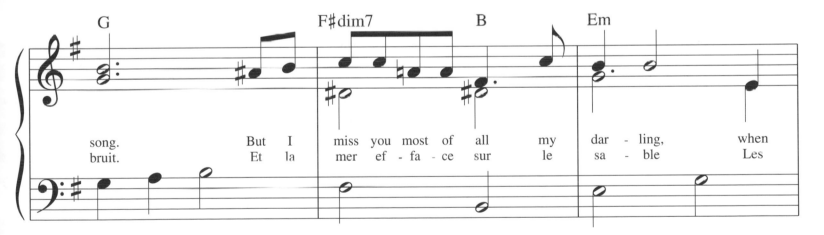

BLUE SKIES
from BETSY

Words and Music by
IRVING BERLIN

Medium Swing

Blue skies _____ smil - ing at me. _____
Blue birds _____ sing - ing a song. _____

_____ Noth - ing but blue skies _____ do I
_____ Noth - ing but blue - birds _____ all day

see.

long.

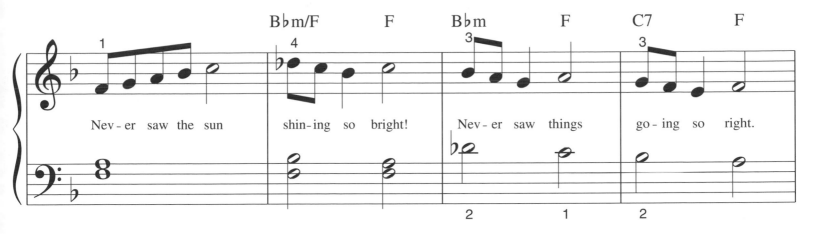

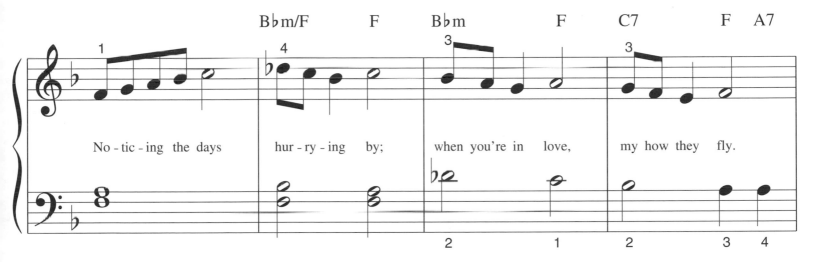

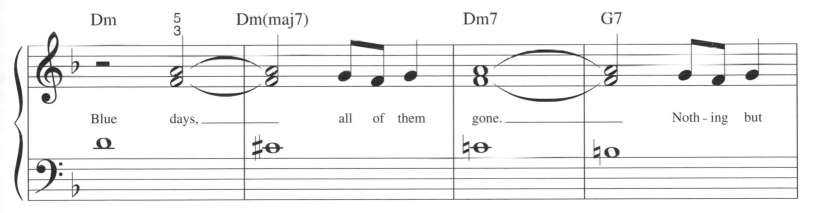

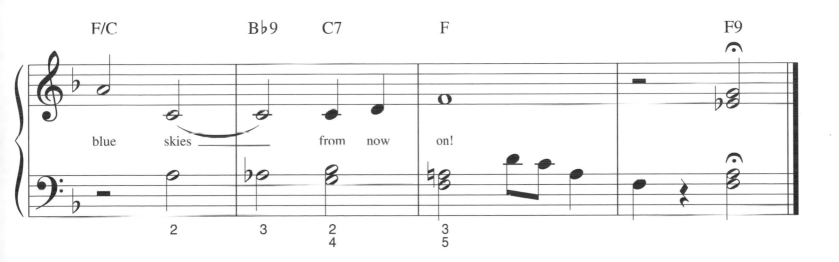

BLUESETTE

Words by NORMAN GIMBEL
Music by JEAN THIELEMANS

Moderately fast Jazz Waltz

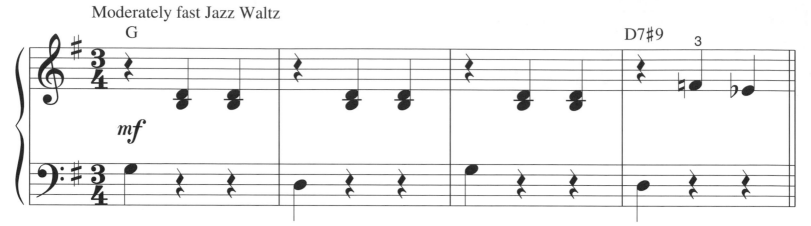

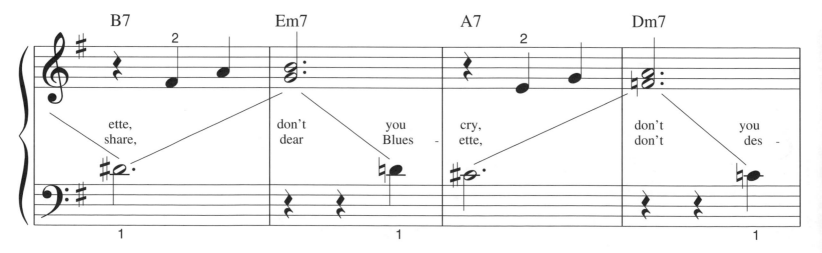

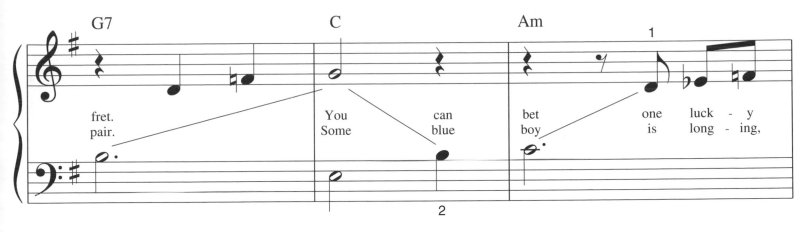

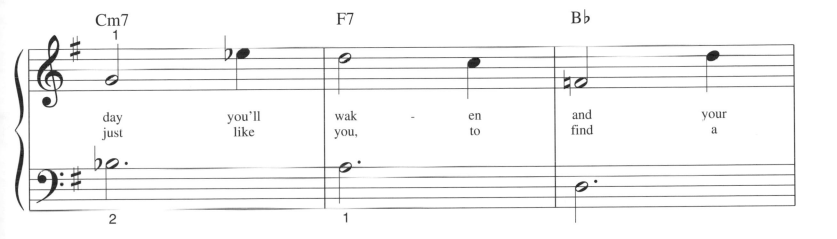

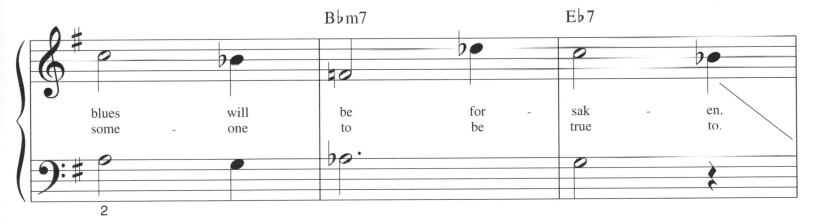

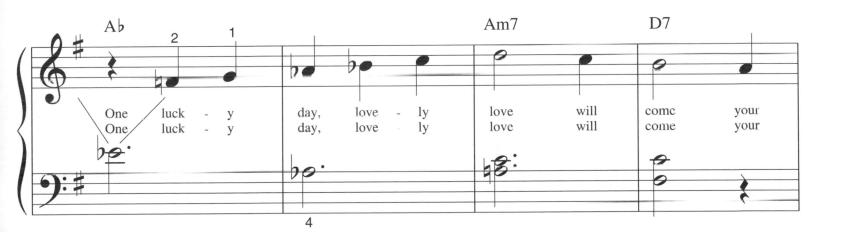

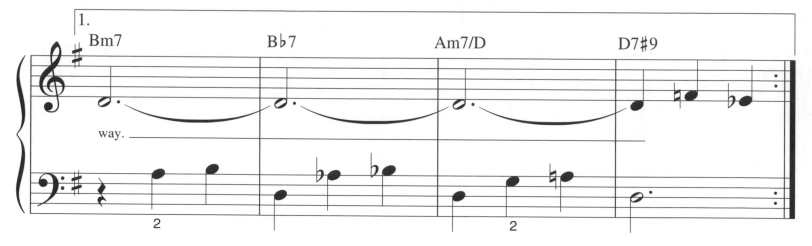

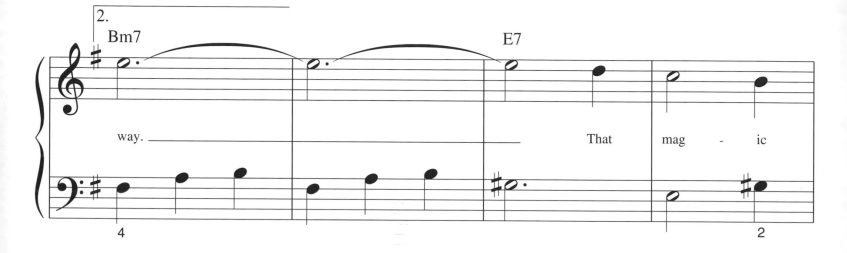

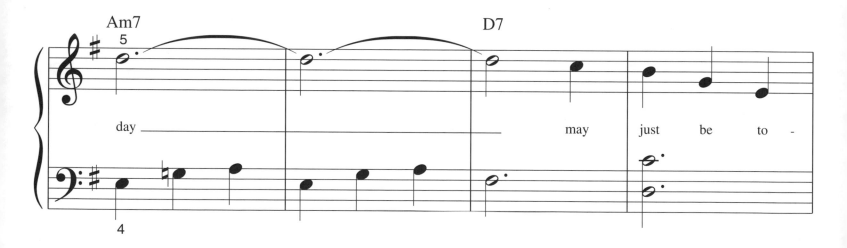

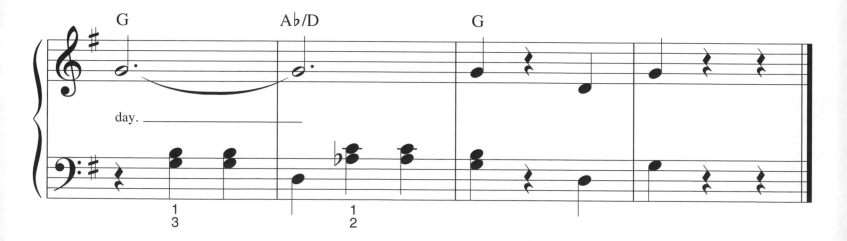

BODY AND SOUL

Words by EDWARD HEYMAN,
ROBERT SOUR and FRANK EYTON
Music by JOHN GREEN

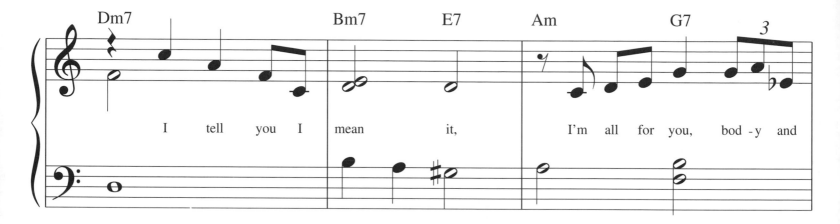

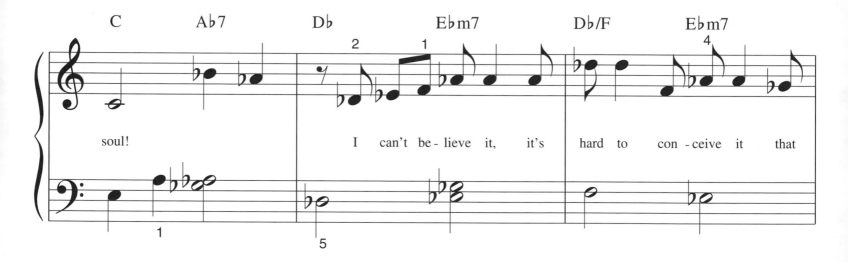

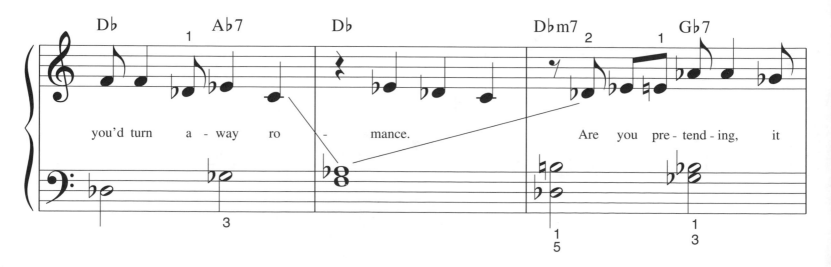

looks like the end -ing un - less I could have one more dance to prove, dear.

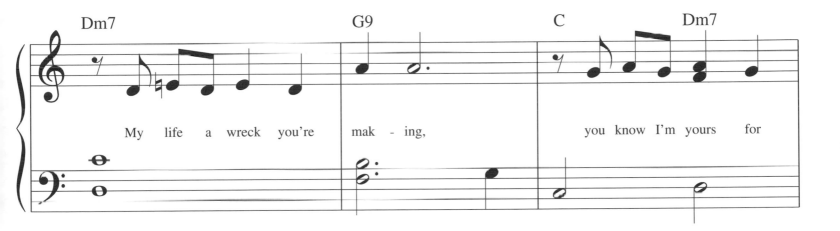

My life a wreck you're mak - ing, you know I'm yours for

just the tak - ing, I'd glad - ly sur - ren - der

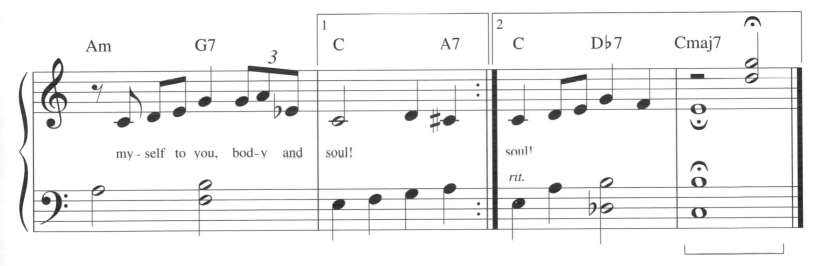

my - self to you, bod - y and soul! soul!

DON'T GET AROUND MUCH ANYMORE

from SOPHISTICATED LADY

Words and Music by DUKE ELLINGTON
and BOB RUSSELL

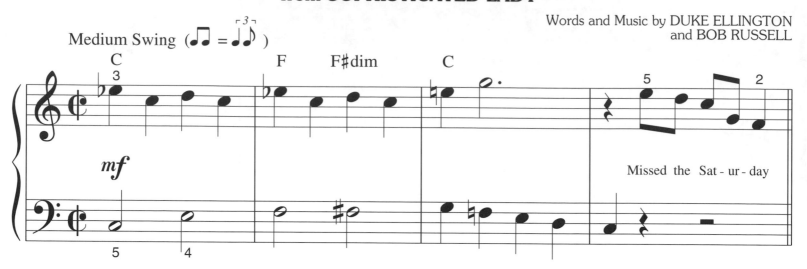

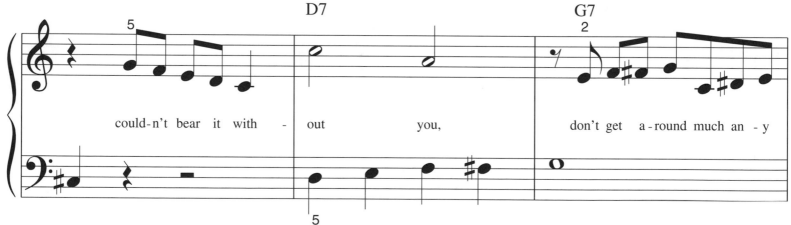

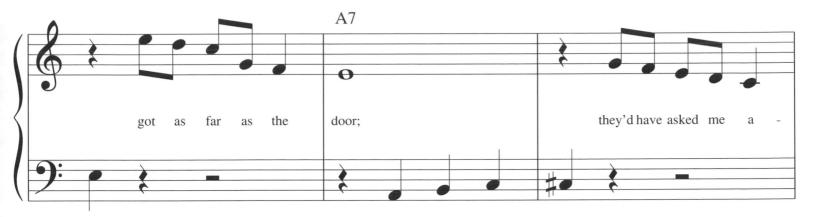

got as far as the door; they'd have asked me a -

bout you, don't get a - round much an - y - more.

Dar - ling, I guess my

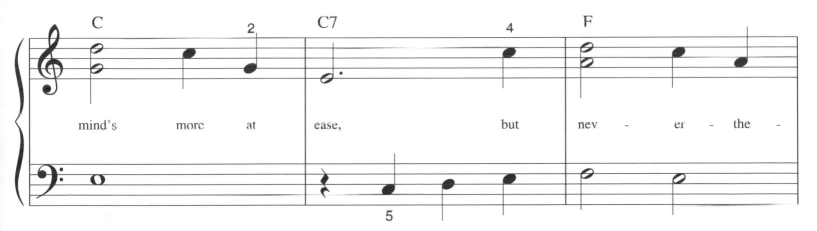

mind's more at ease, but nev - er - the -

D#dim   Em7   G7

less   why stir up mem - o - ries? Been in -vit -ed on

C   A7

dates,   might have gone but what   for?

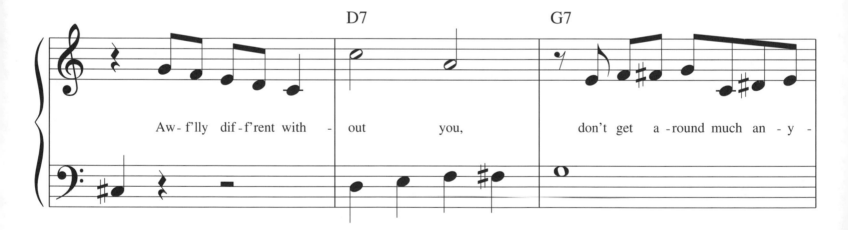

D7   G7

Aw- f'lly dif -f'rent with - out   you,   don't get a -round much an -y -

1. C   2. C

more.   Missed the Sat -ur -day   more.

IN A SENTIMENTAL MOOD

Words and Music by DUKE ELLINGTON,
IRVING MILLS and MANNY KURTZ

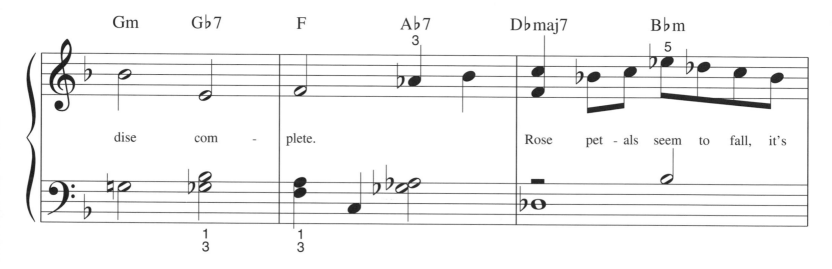

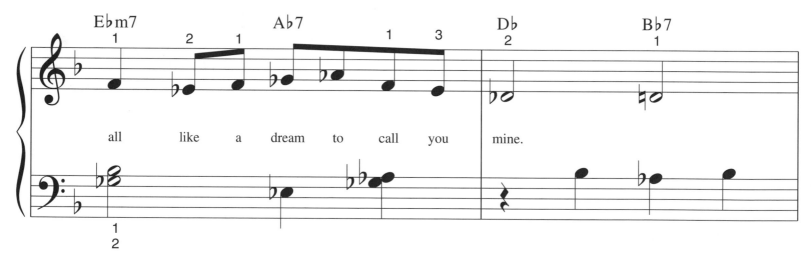

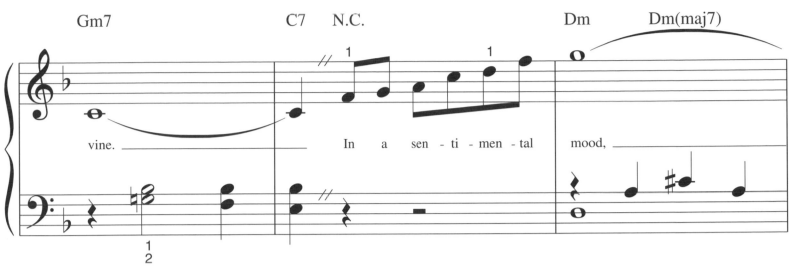

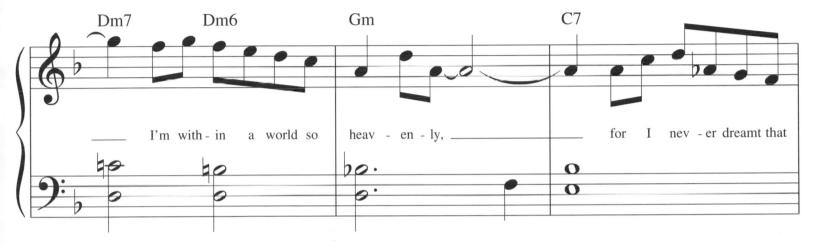

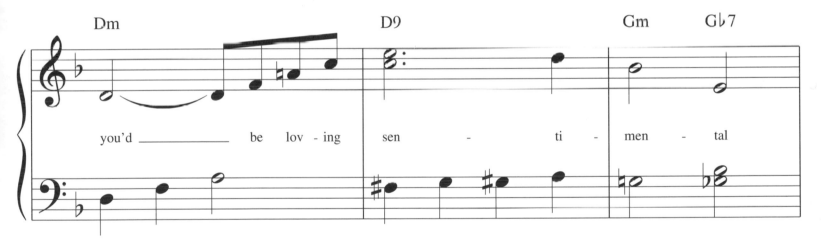

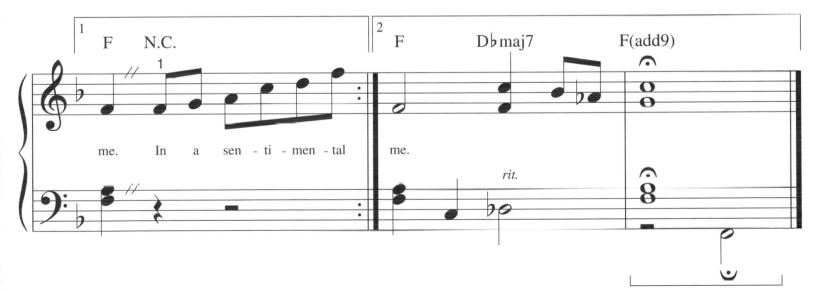

I'LL REMEMBER APRIL

Words and Music by PAT JOHNSON, DON RAYE and GENE DE PAUL

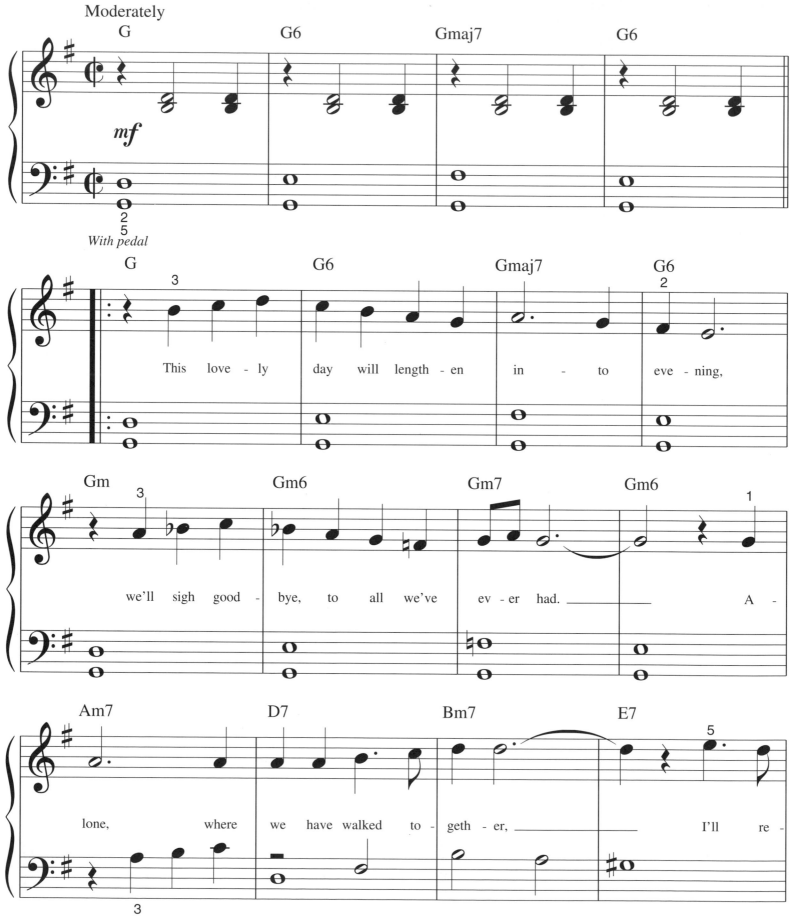

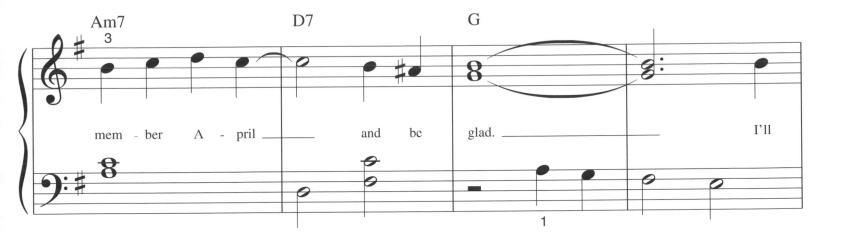

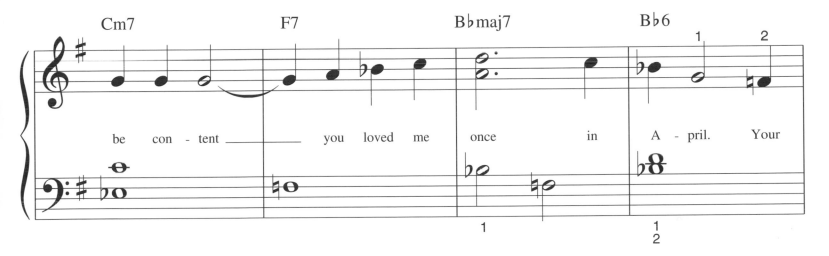

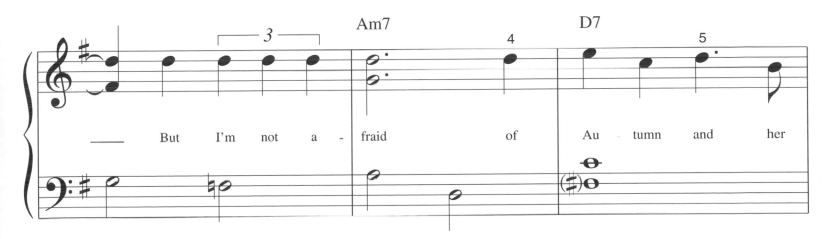

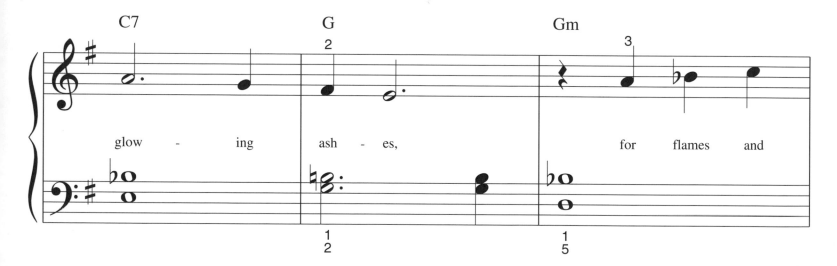

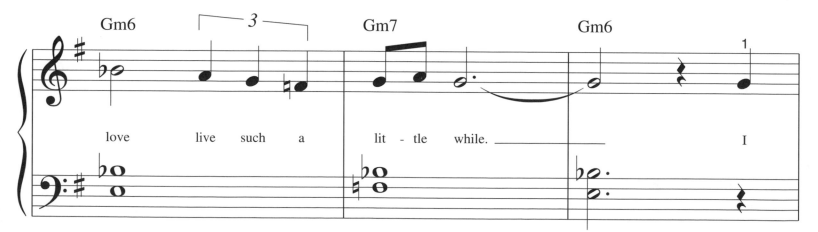

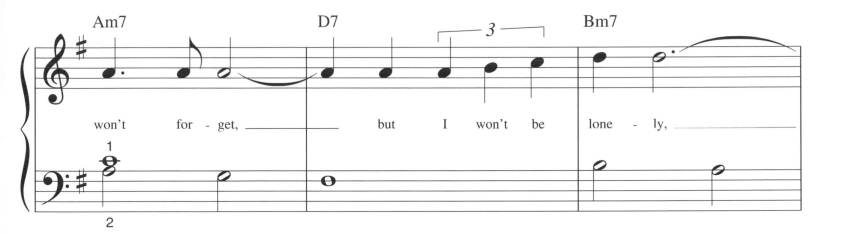

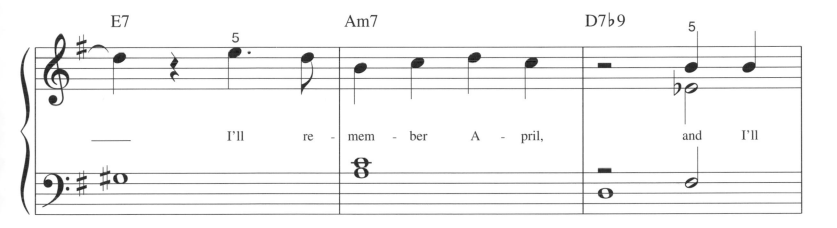

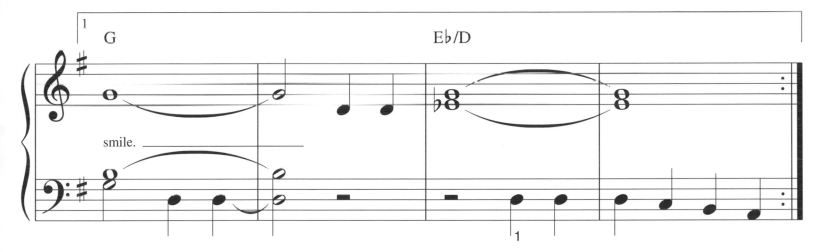

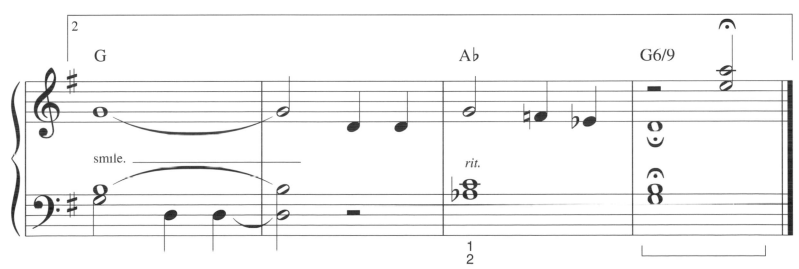

MOOD INDIGO
from SOPHISTICATED LADIES

Words and Music by DUKE ELLINGTON,
IRVING MILLS and ALBANY BIGARD

Medium Slow Swing

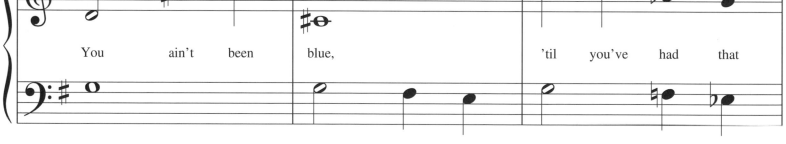

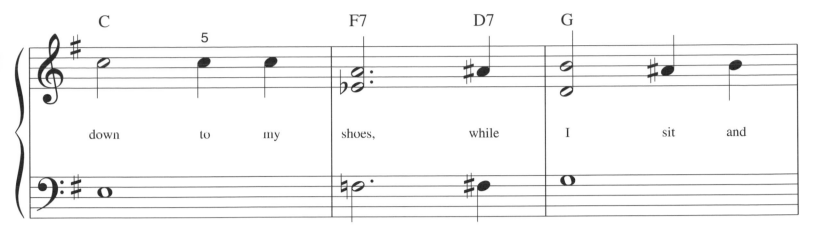

down   to   my   shoes,   while   I   sit   and

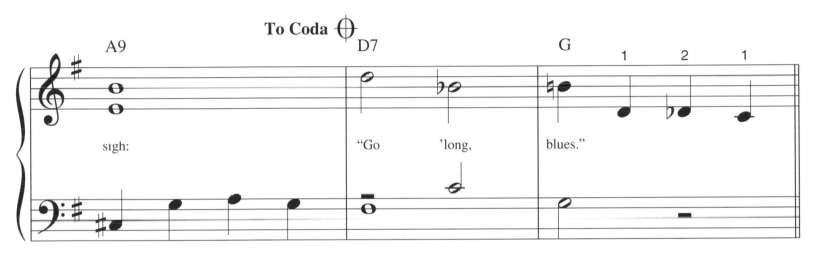

sigh: "Go   'long,   blues."

Al - ways get   that   mood in - di - go, ___   since my ba - by said good -

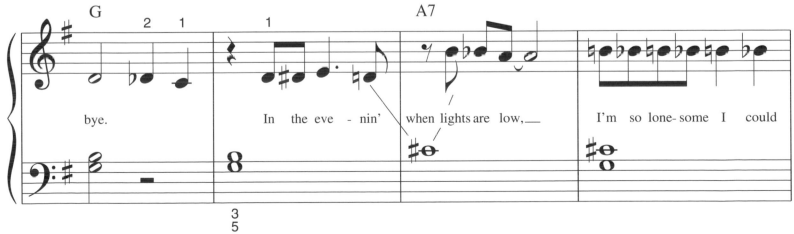

bye.   In the eve - nin'   when lights are low, ___   I'm so lone-some I could

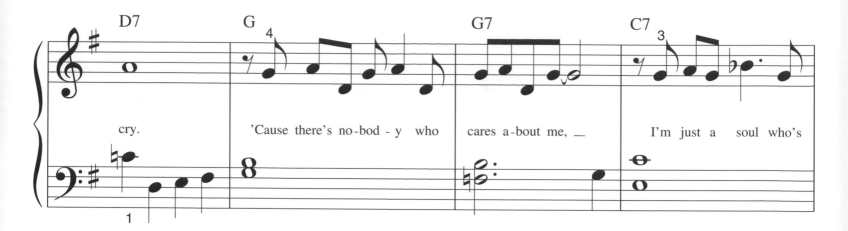

'cry. | 'Cause there's no-bod-y who | cares a-bout me, — | I'm just a soul who's

blu-er than blue can be. | When I get that | mood in-di-go, —

Am7 ... D7 | 1. G | 2. G Cm6 D7 — D.S. al Coda

I could lay me down and | die. | die.

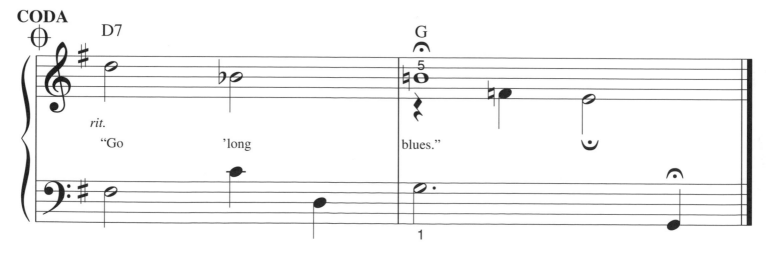

CODA

rit.
"Go 'long blues."

MY ROMANCE
from JUMBO

Words by LORENZ HART
Music by RICHARD RODGERS

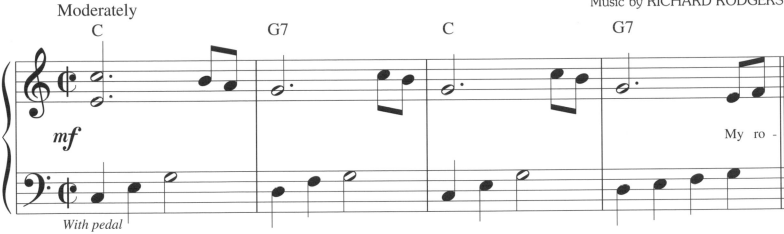

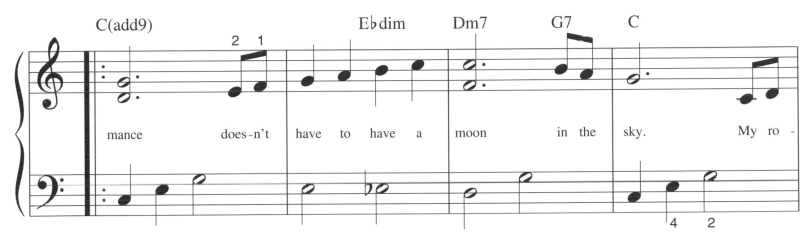

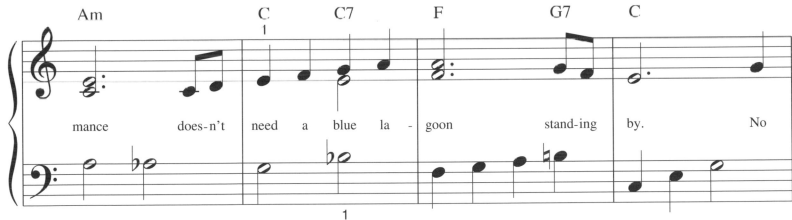

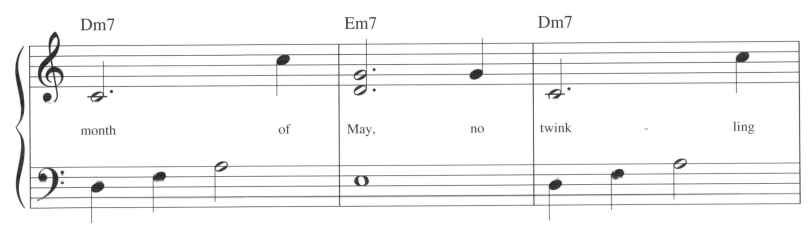

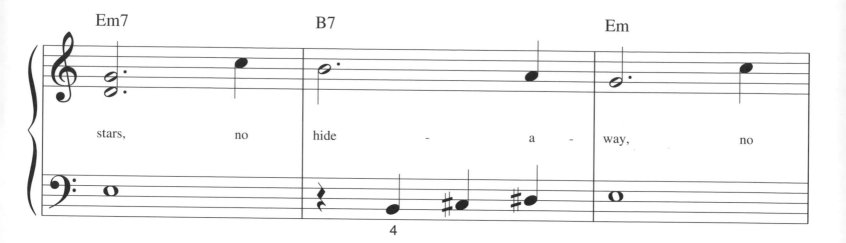

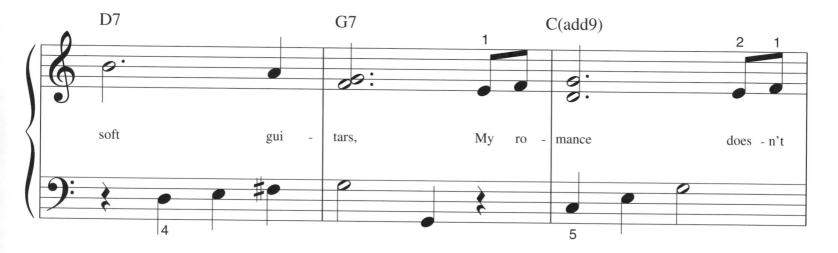

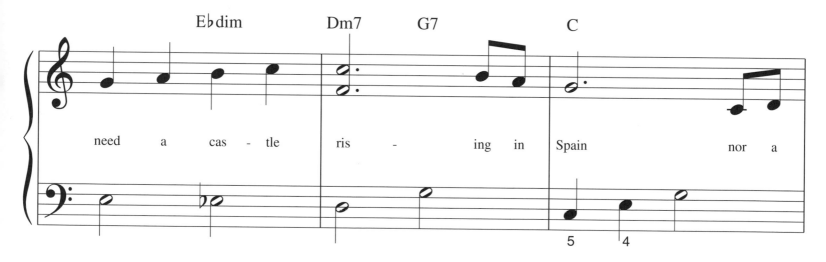

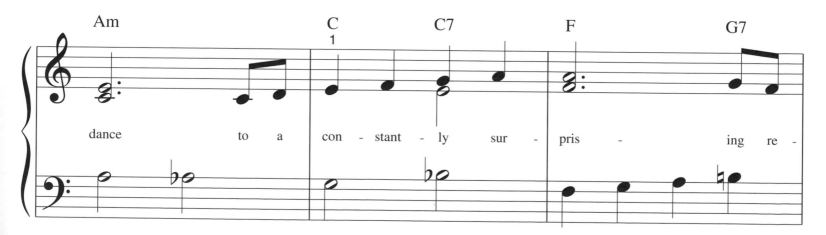

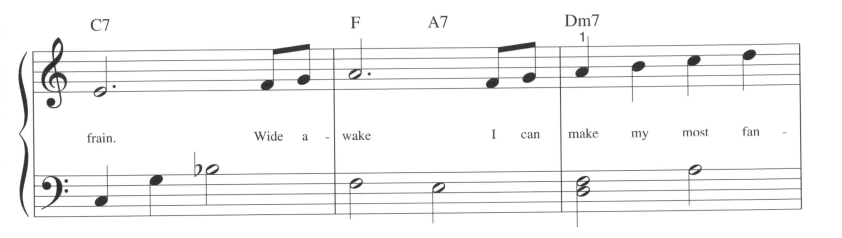

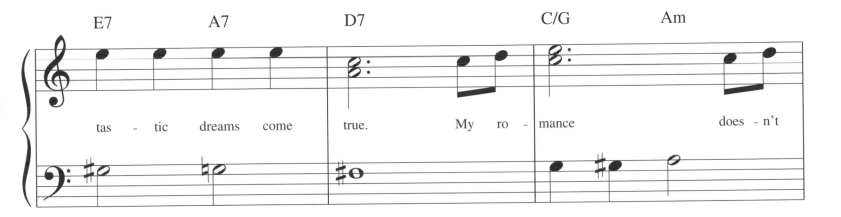

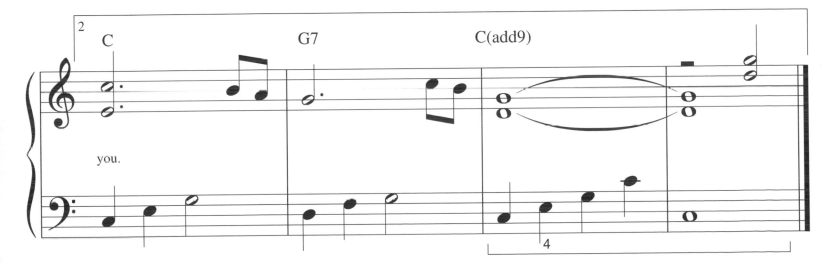

MY FAVORITE THINGS
from THE SOUND OF MUSIC

Lyrics by OSCAR HAMMERSTEIN II
Music by RICHARD RODGERS

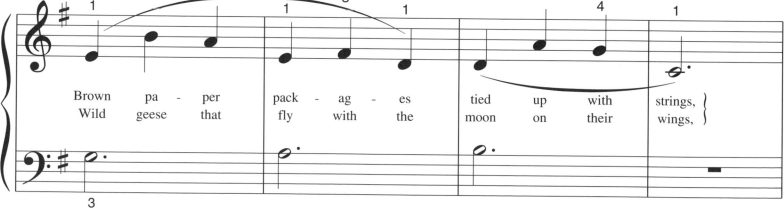

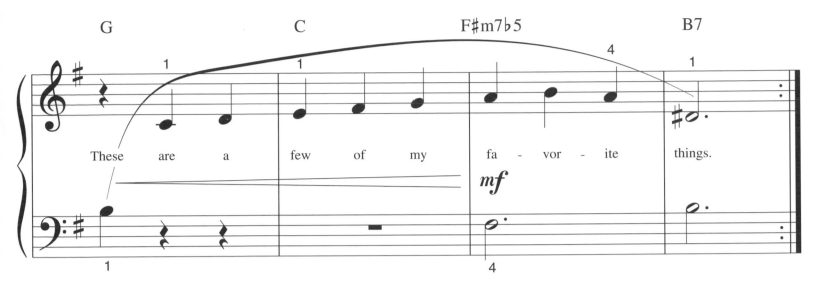

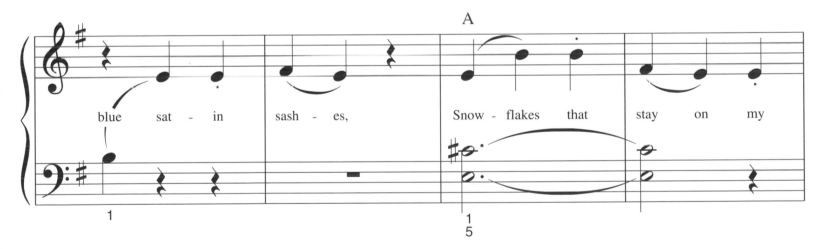

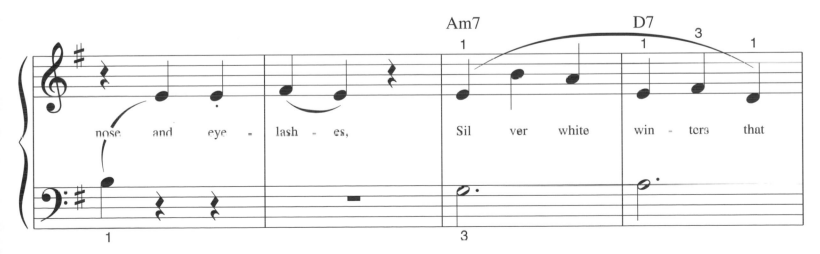

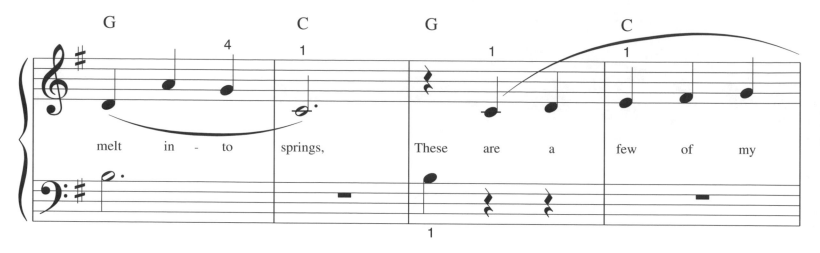

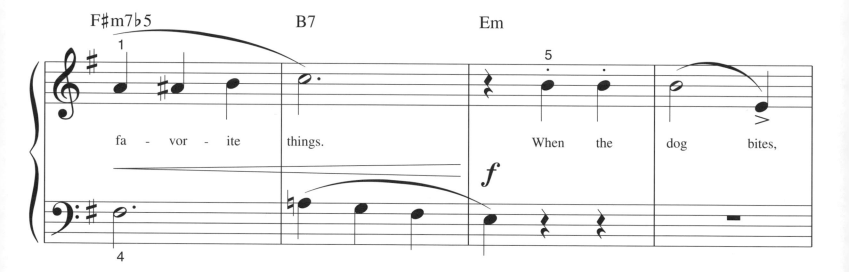

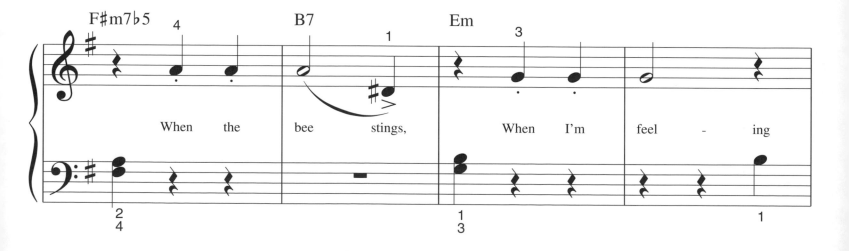

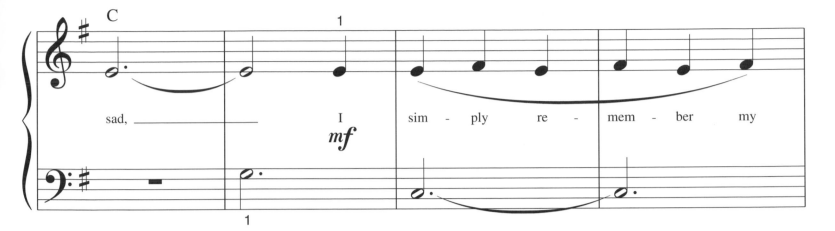

sad, _____ I sim - ply re - mem - ber my

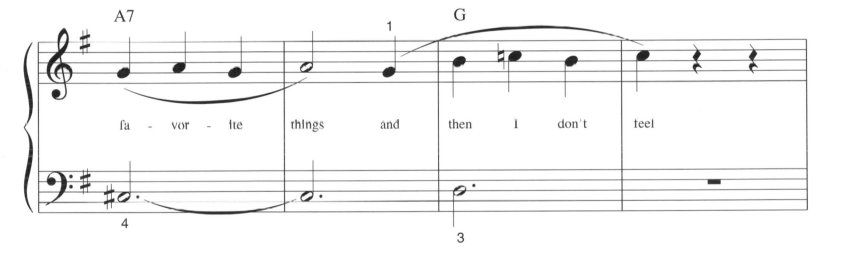

fa - vor - ite things and then I don't feel

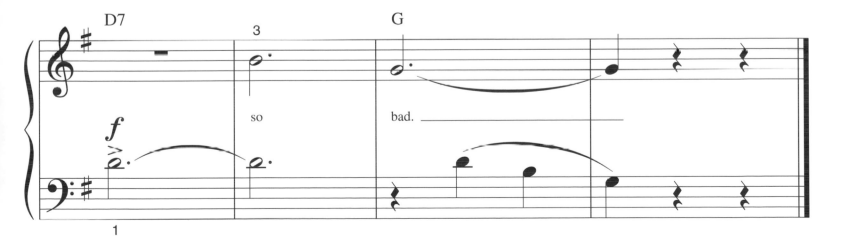

so bad. _____

MY FUNNY VALENTINE

from BABES IN ARMS

Words by LORENZ HART
Music by RICHARD RODGERS

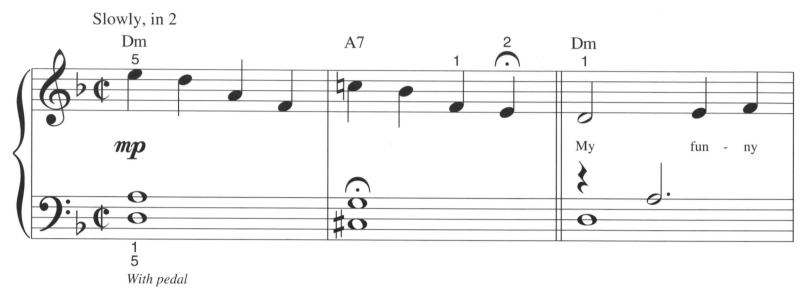

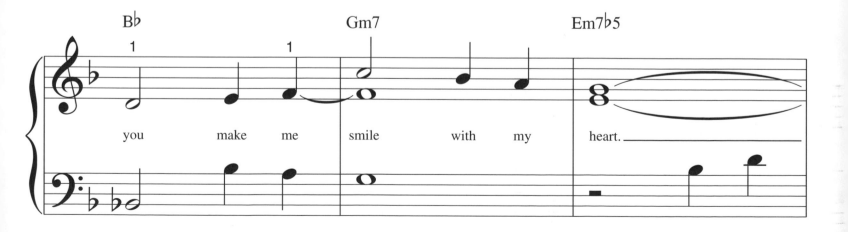

Your looks are laugh - a - ble,

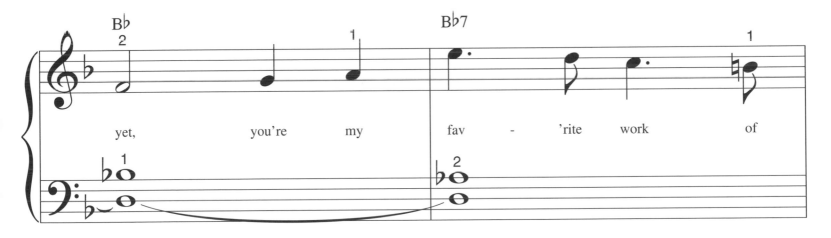

un - pho - to - graph - a - ble,

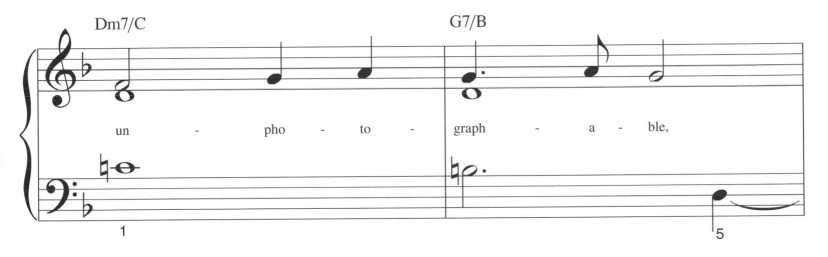

yet, you're my fav - 'rite work of

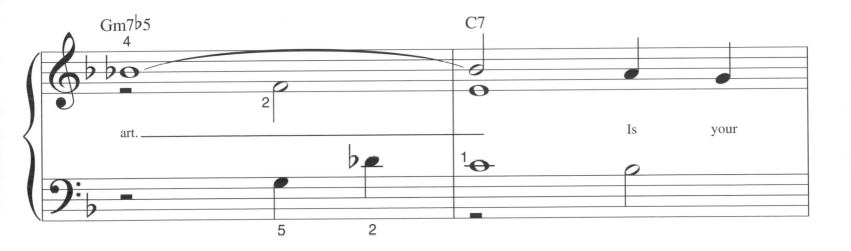

art. ___ Is your

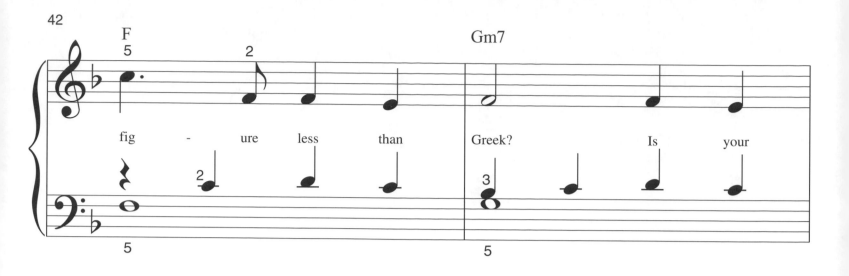

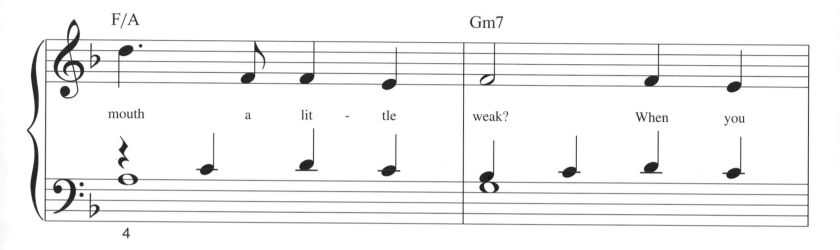

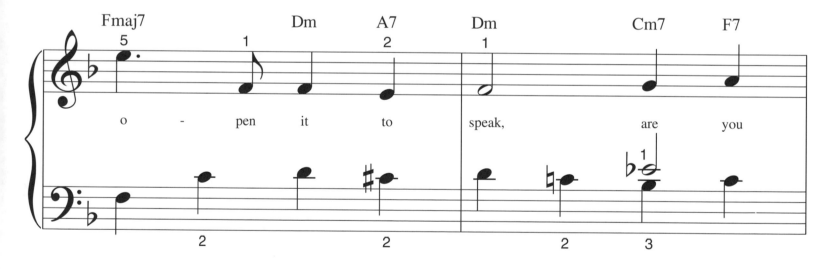

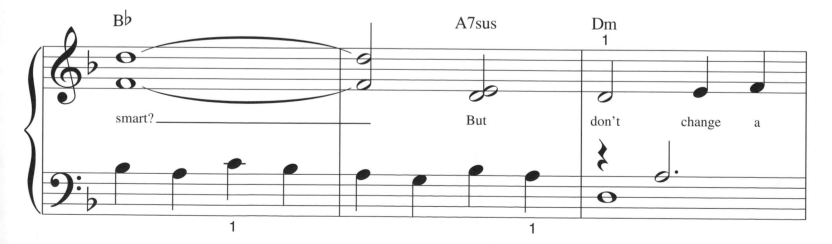

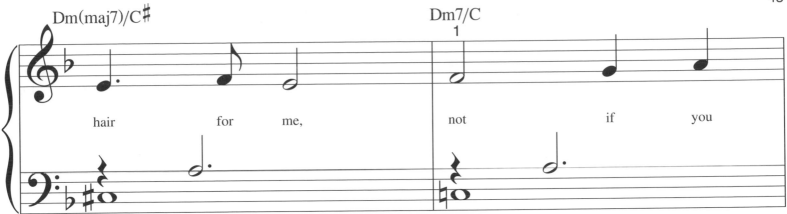

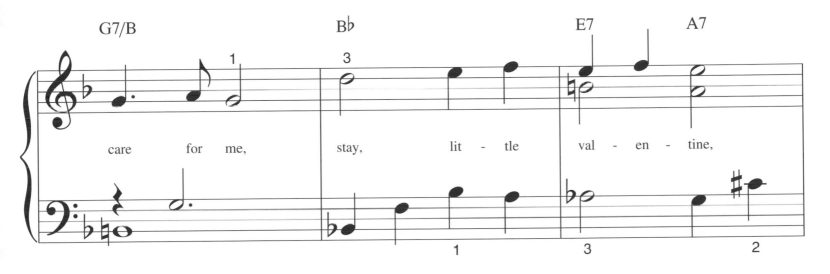

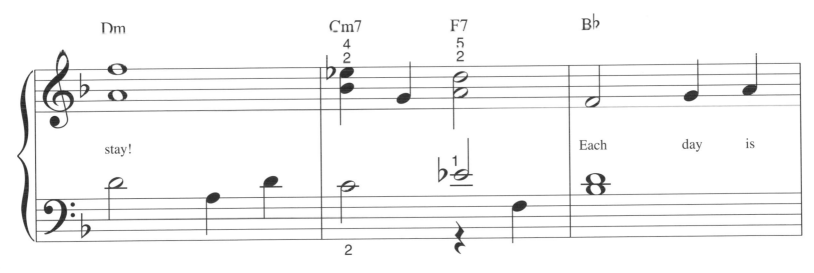

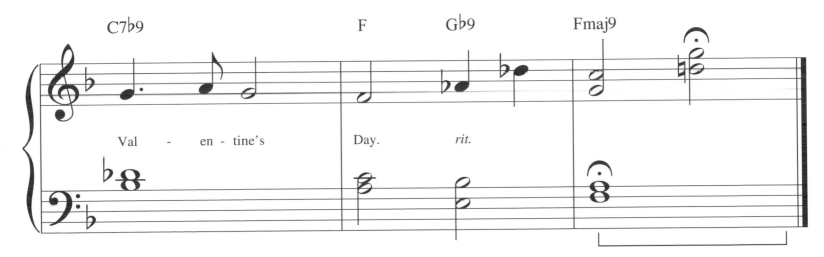

THE NEARNESS OF YOU

from the Paramount Picture ROMANCE IN THE DARK

Words by NED WASHINGTON
Music by HOAGY CARMICHAEL

Slowly

45

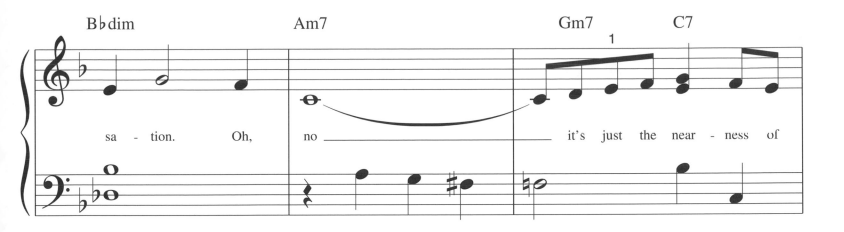

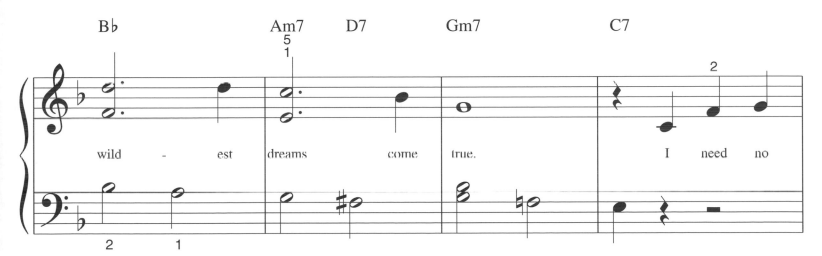

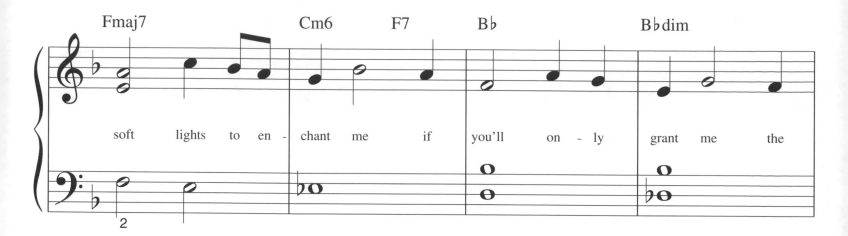

soft lights to en - chant me if you'll on - ly grant me the

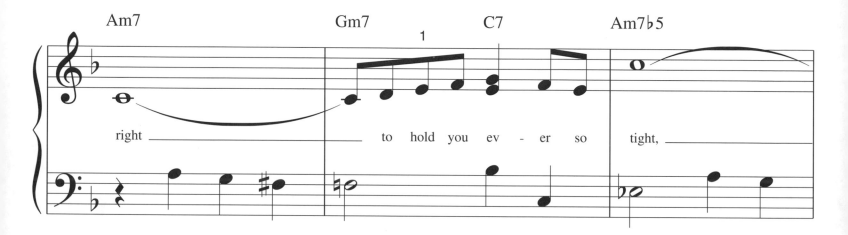

right _____ to hold you ev - er so tight, _____

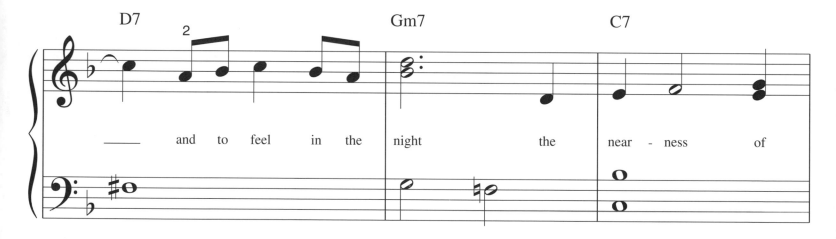

_____ and to feel in the night the near - ness of

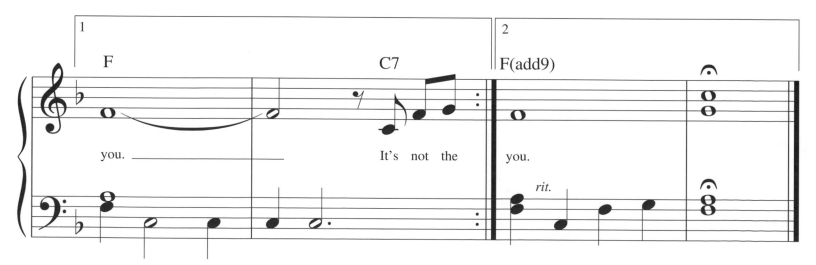

you. _____ It's not the you.

SATIN DOLL
from SOPHISTICATED LADIES

Words by JOHNNY MERCER and BILLY STRAYHORN
Music by DUKE ELLINGTON

Cig - a - rette hold - er

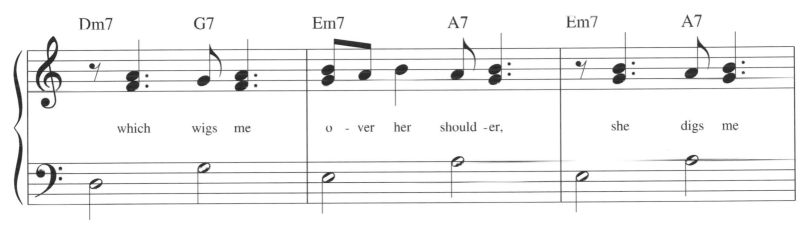

which wigs me   o - ver her should -er,   she digs me

Out   cat - tin'   that   sat - in   doll.

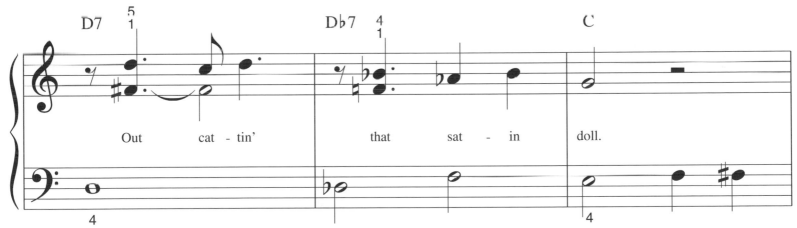

Ba - by shall   we   go   out   skip - pin'

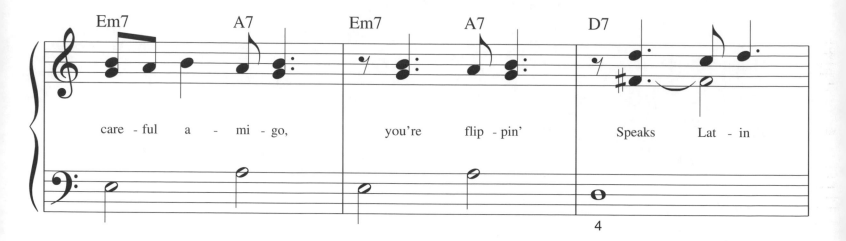

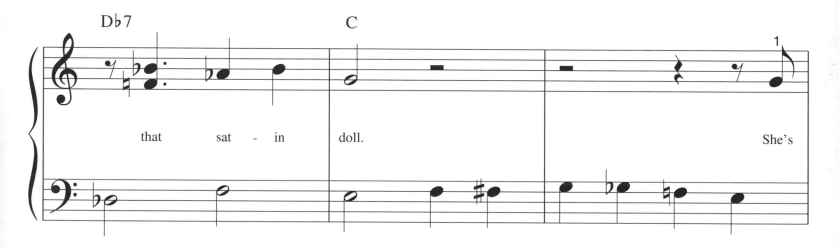

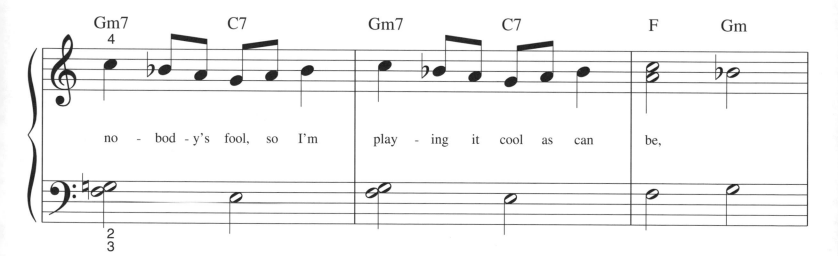

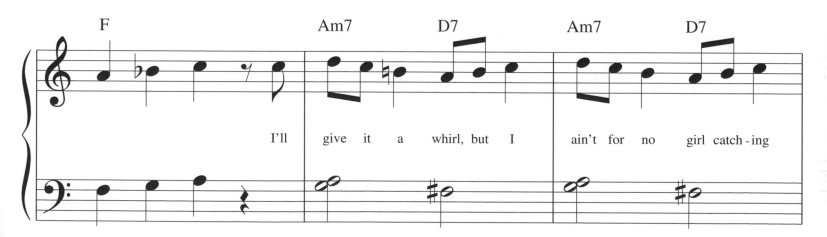

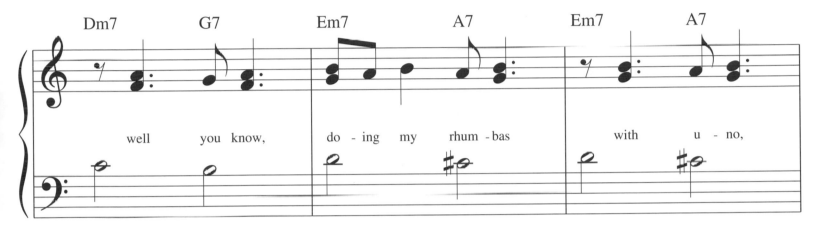

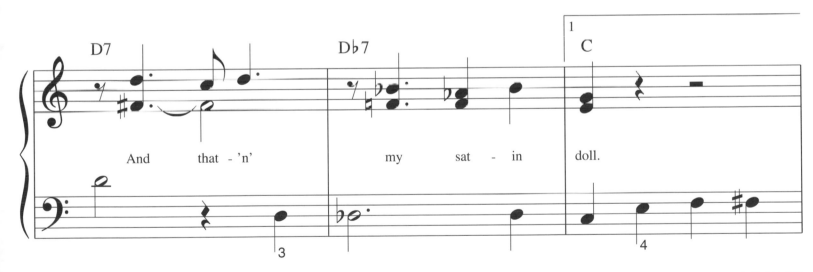

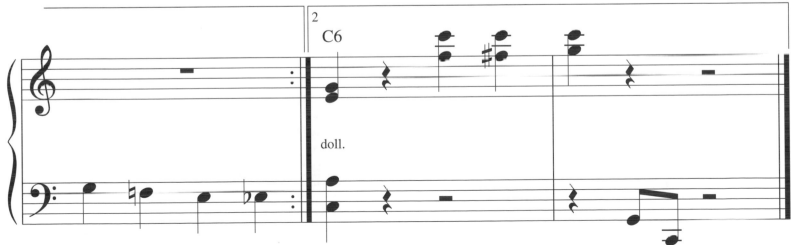

STELLA BY STARLIGHT
from the Paramount Picture THE UNINVITED

Words by NED WASHINGTON
Music by VICTOR YOUNG

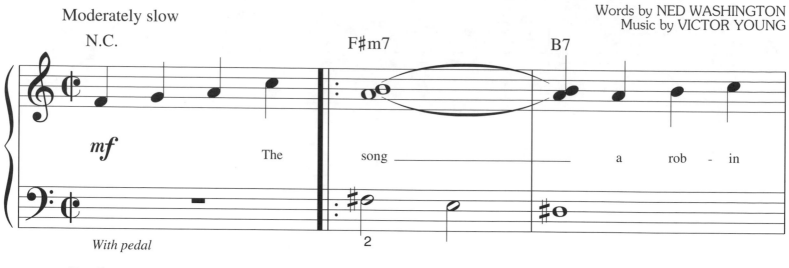

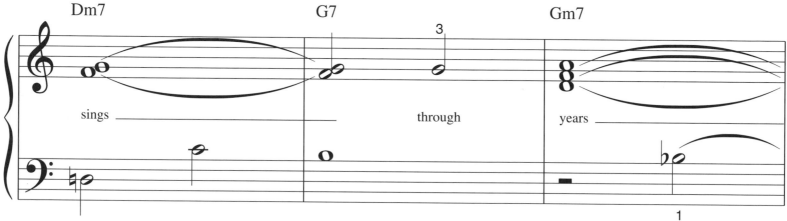

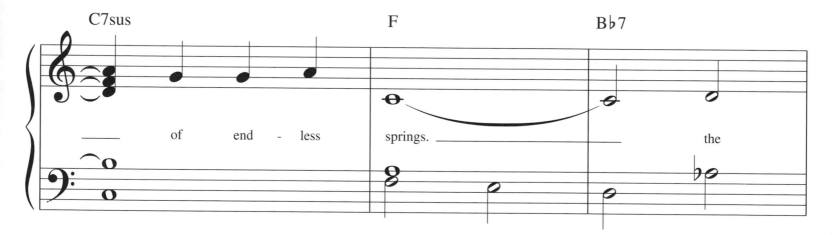

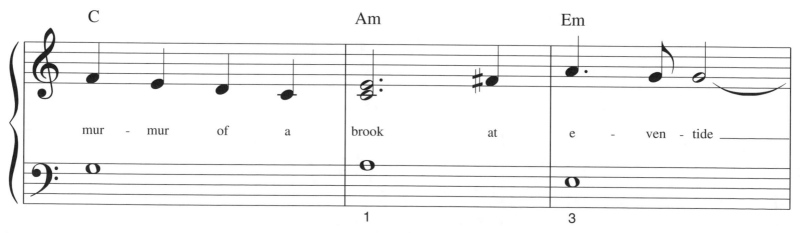

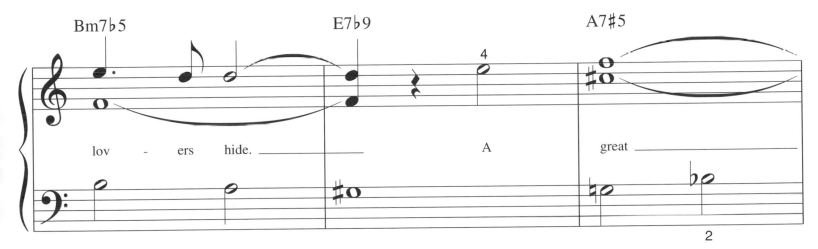

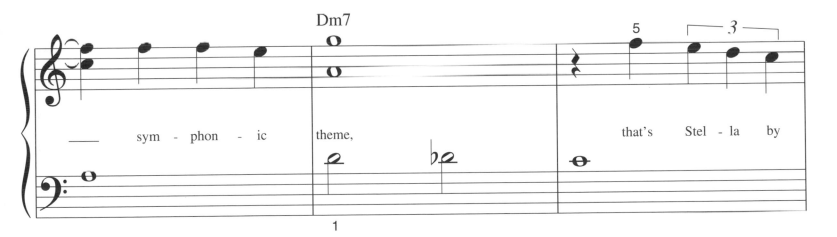

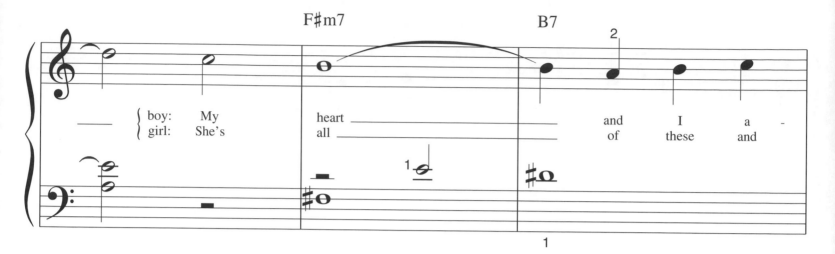

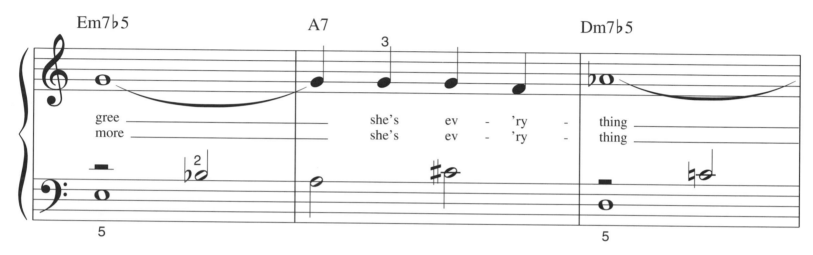

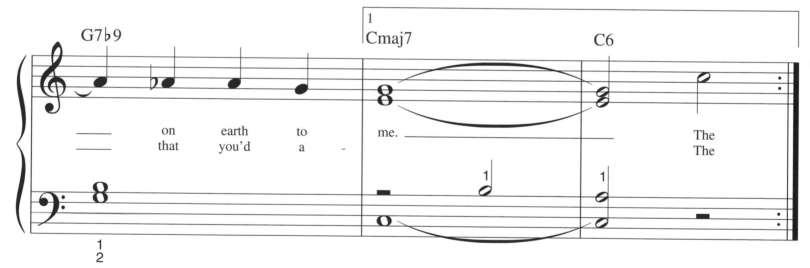

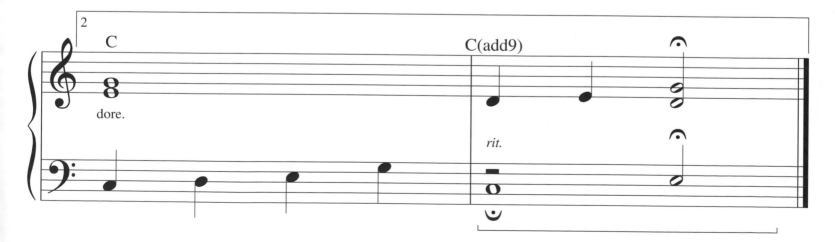

TANGERINE
from the Paramount Picture THE FLEET'S IN

Words by JOHNNY MERCER
Music by VICTOR SCHERTZINGER

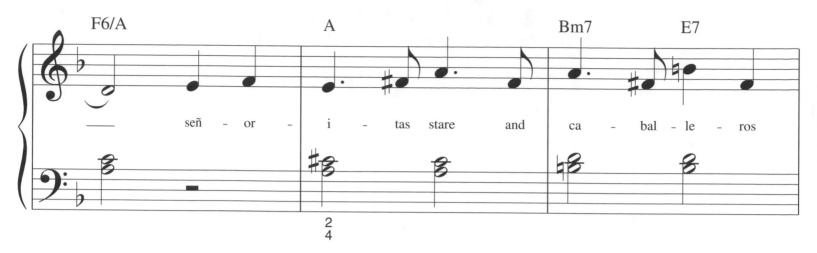

señ - or - i - tas stare and ca - bal - le - ros

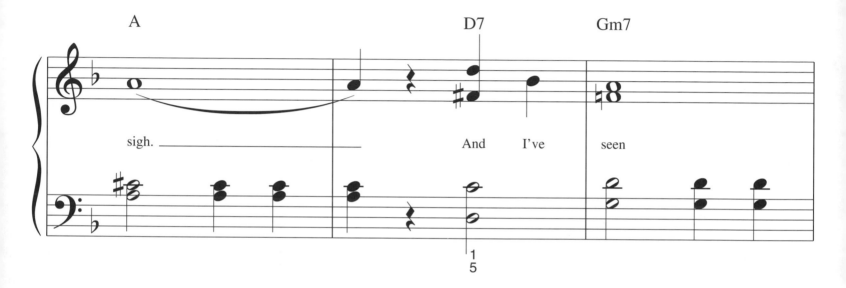

sigh. _____ And I've seen

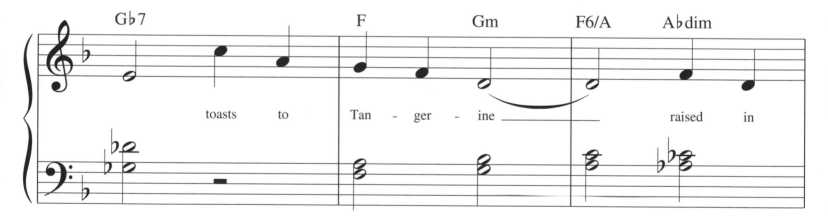

toasts to Tan - ger - ine _____ raised in

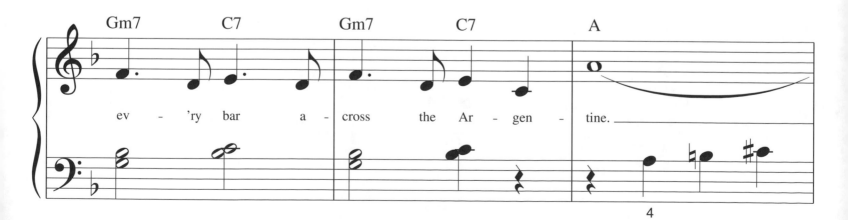

ev - 'ry bar a - cross the Ar - gen - tine. _____

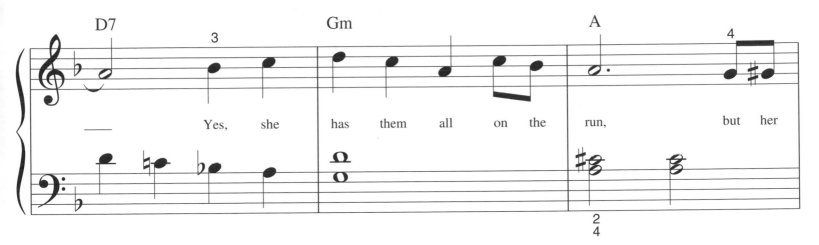

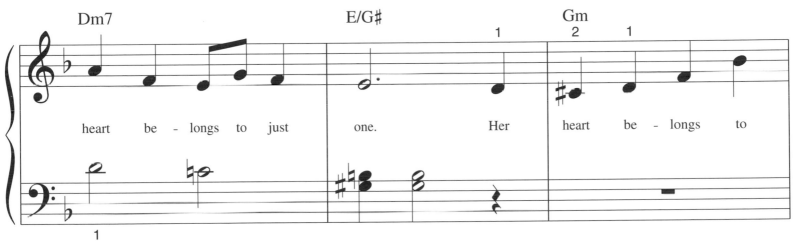

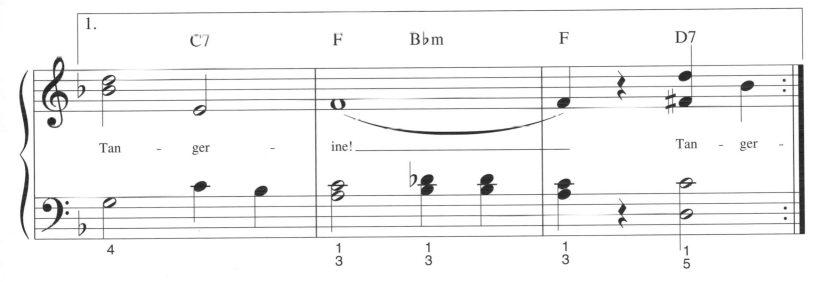

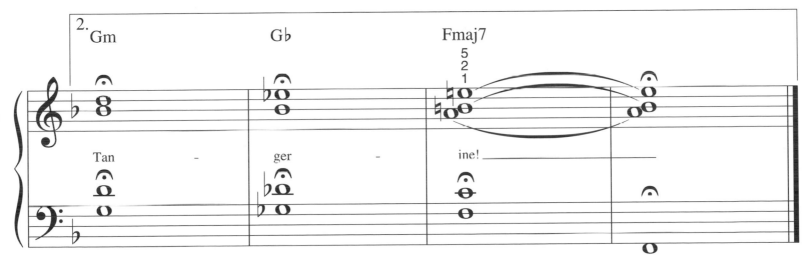

THE VERY THOUGHT OF YOU

Words and Music by
RAY NOBLE

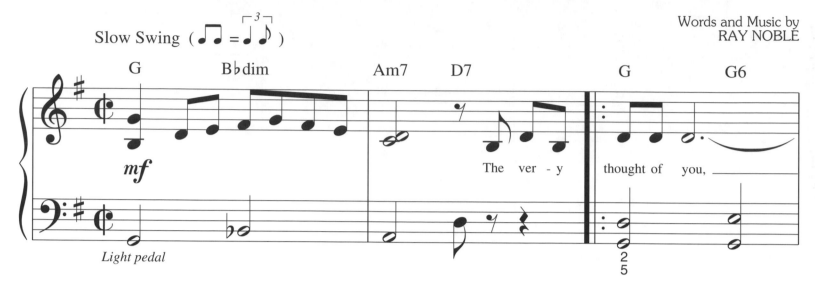

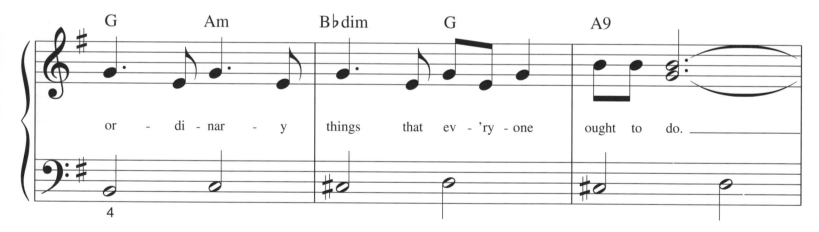

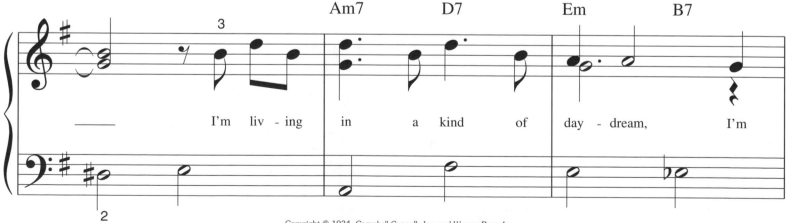

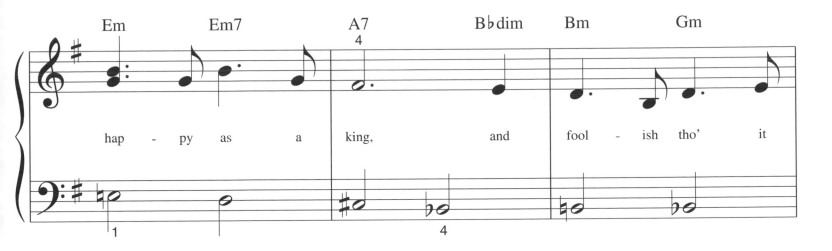

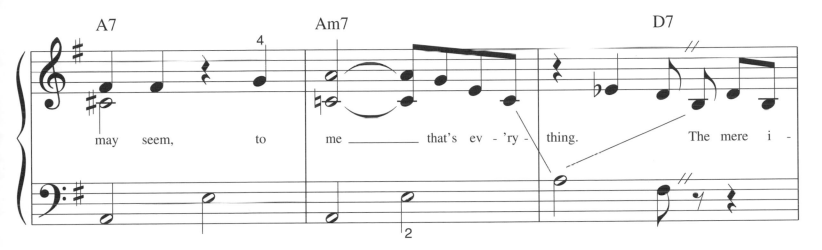

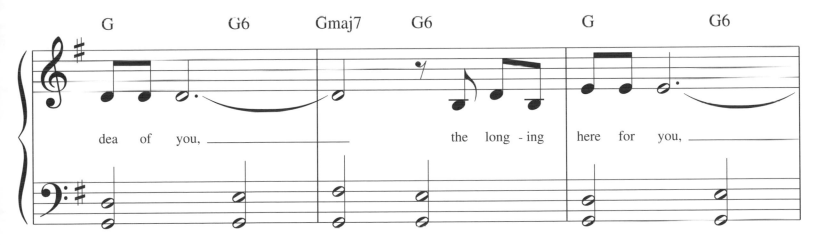

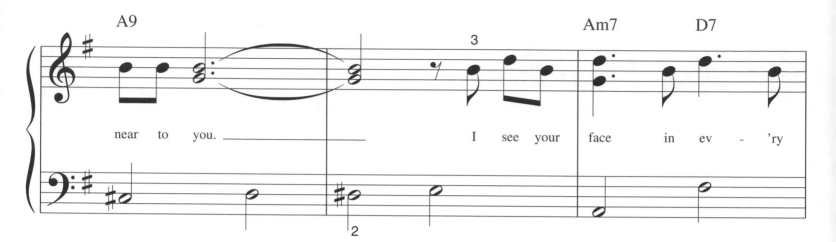

near to you. _____ I see your face in ev - 'ry

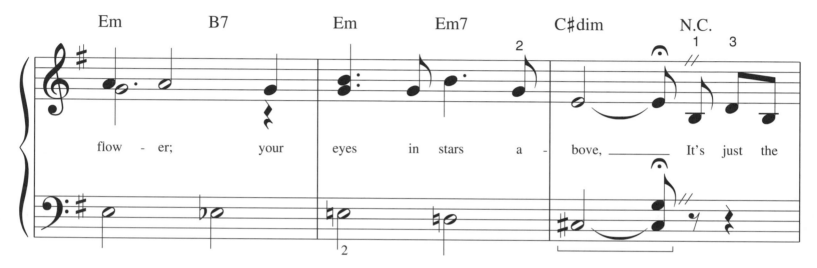

flow - er; your eyes in stars a - bove, _____ It's just the

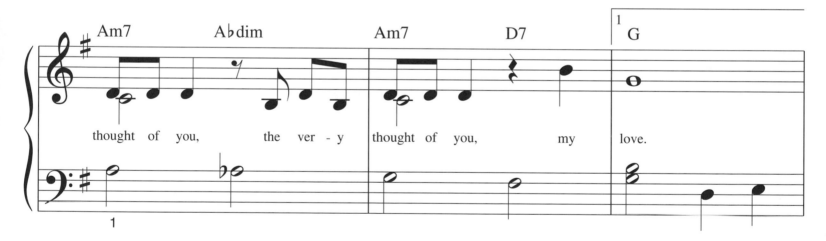

thought of you, the ver - y thought of you, my love.

The ver - y love.

rit.

WHEN I FALL IN LOVE

from ONE MINUTE TO ZERO

Words by EDWARD HEYMAN
Music by VICTOR YOUNG

Slowly

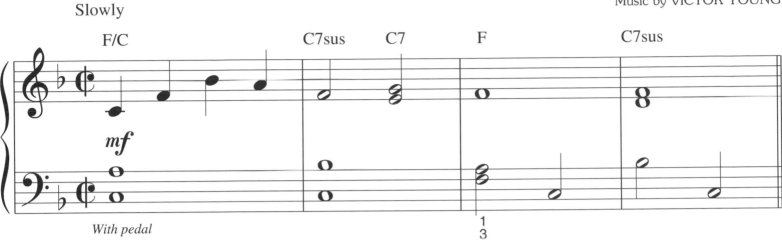

With pedal

When I fall in love it will be for - ev - er,

or I'll nev - er fall in love. In a

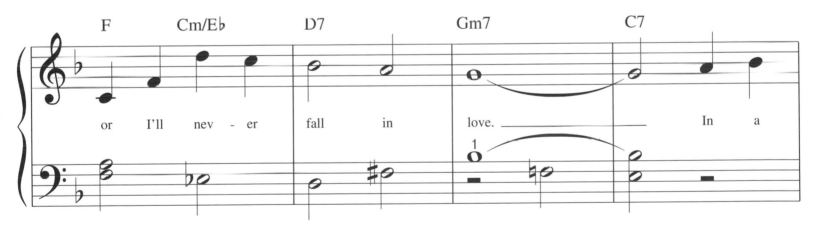

rest - less world like this is, love is end - ed be - fore it's be -

60

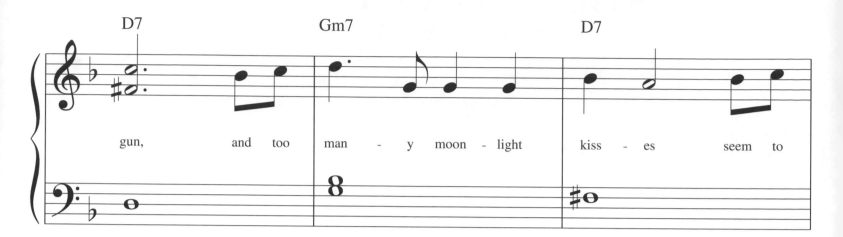

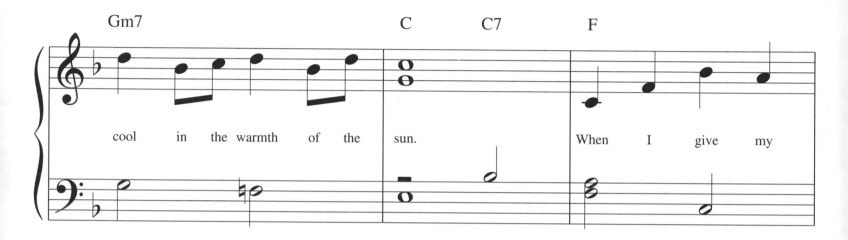

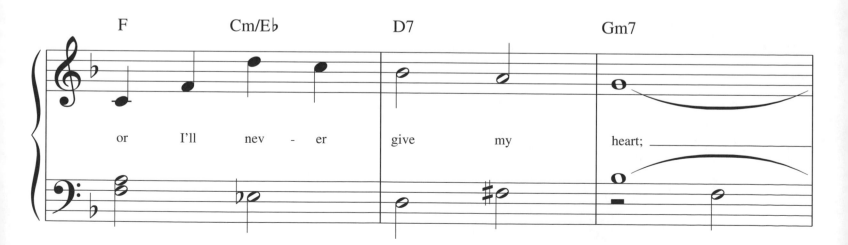

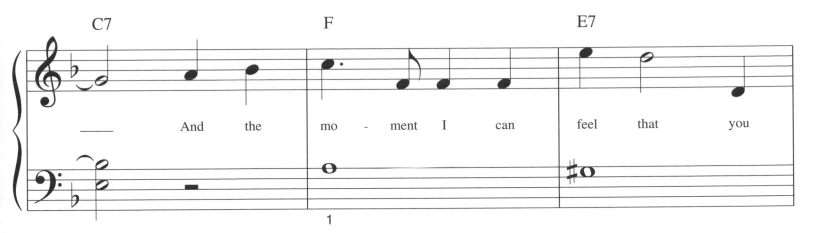

C7   F   E7

And the mo - ment I can feel that you

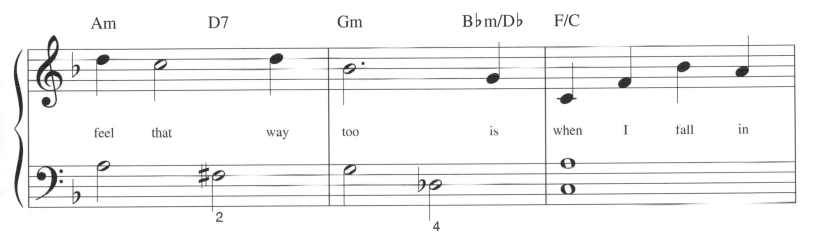

Am   D7   Gm   B♭m/D♭   F/C

feel that way too is when I fall in

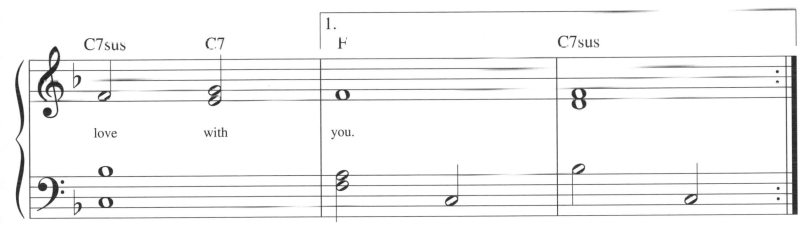

C7sus   C7   1. F   C7sus

love with you.

2. F   C7sus   F   E♭   Fmaj7

you.

WHEN SUNNY GETS BLUE

Lyric by JACK SEGAL
Music by MARVIN FISHER

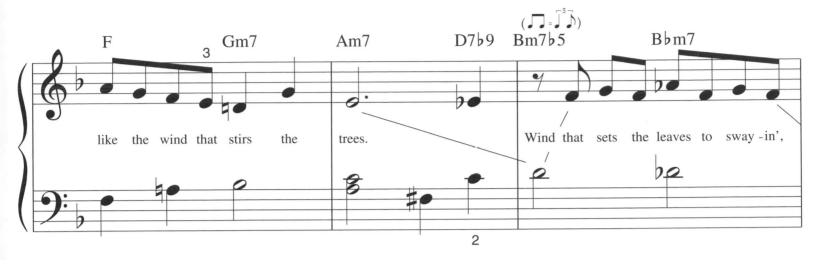

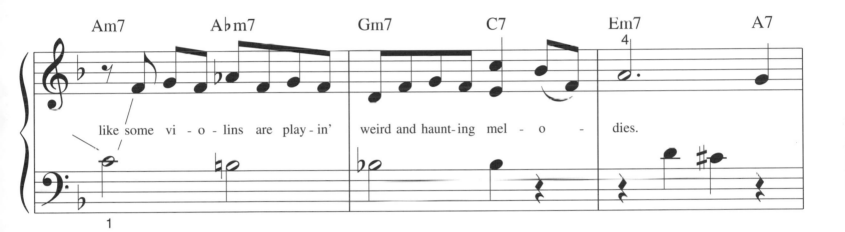

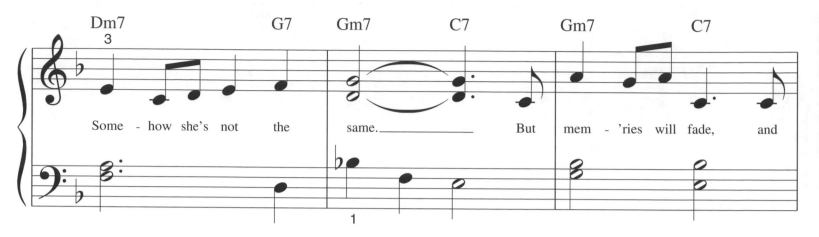

Some - how she's not the same._____ But mem - 'ries will fade, and

pret - ty dreams will rise up where her oth - er dream fell through.

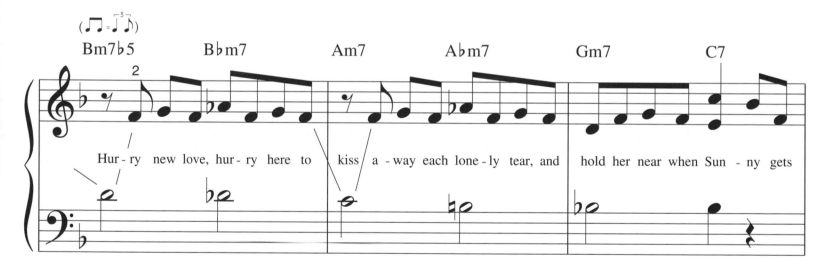

Hur - ry new love, hur - ry here to kiss a - way each lone - ly tear, and hold her near when Sun - ny gets

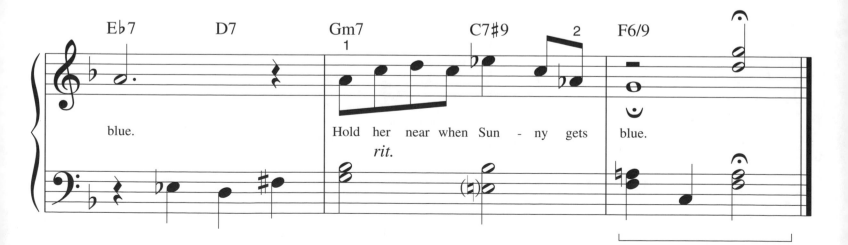

blue. Hold her near when Sun - ny gets blue.

rit.